the invisible art of literary editing

the invisible art of literary editing

BRYAN FURUNESS AND SARAH LAYDEN

BLOOMSBURY ACADEMIC

LONDON • NEW YORK • OXFORD • NEW DELHI • SYDNEY

BLOOMSBURY ACADEMIC
Bloomsbury Publishing Plc
50 Bedford Square, London, WC1B 3DP, UK
1385 Broadway, New York, NY 10018, USA
29 Earlsfort Terrace, Dublin 2, Ireland

BLOOMSBURY, BLOOMSBURY ACADEMIC and the Diana logo are trademarks of
Bloomsbury Publishing Plc

First published in Great Britain 2023

A catalogue record for this book is available from the British Library.

Library of Congress Cataloging-in-Publication Data Names: Furuness, Bryan,
author. | Layden, Sarah, author. Title: The invisible art of literary editing /
Bryan Furuness and Sarah Layden. Description: London ; New York :
Bloomsbury Academic, 2023. | Includes bibliographical references.
Identifiers: LCCN 2022041494 (print) | LCCN 2022041495 (ebook) | ISBN 9781350296480
(paperback) | ISBN 9781350296473 (hardback) | ISBN 9781350296497 (pdf) | ISBN
9781350296503 (epub) Subjects: LCSH: Editing. Classification: LCC PN162 .F87 2023
(print) | LCC PN162 (ebook) | DDC 808.02/7–dc23/eng/20220926 LC record available at
https://lccn.loc.gov/2022041494
LC ebook record available at https://lccn.loc.gov/2022041495

ISBN: HB: 978-1-3502-9647-3
        PB: 978-1-3502-9648-0
        ePDF: 978-1-3502-9649-7
        ePub: 978-1-3502-9650-3

Typeset by RefineCatch Limited, Bungay, Suffolk
Printed and bound in Great Britain

To find out more about our authors and books visit www.bloomsbury.com
and sign up for our newsletters.

For our students

Contents

Authors

Bryan Furuness has edited for *Booth*, *On Earth as It Is*, Pressgang, and Engine Books. He is the co-editor (with Michael Martone) of the anthology *Winesburg, Indiana*, and the editor of *An Indiana Christmas* and *My Name was Never Frankenstein: And Other Classic Adventure Tales Remixed*.

Sometimes he writes his own stuff, too. He is the author of a couple of novels, *The Lost Episodes of Revie Bryson* and *Do Not Go On*. His stories have appeared in *New Stories from the Midwest* and *Best American Nonrequired Reading*. He is a Writer in Residence at Butler University, where he has served as the faculty advisor for *Manuscripts*, the undergraduate literary magazine.

Sarah Layden is the author of the books *Imagine Your Life Like This* and *Trip Through Your Wires*, and a flash fiction chapbook, *The Story I Tell Myself About Myself*. Her recent fiction appears in *Boston Review*, *Blackbird*, *Booth*, *Zone 3*, and *Best Microfiction 2020*, with essays and articles in *The Washington Post*, *Poets & Writers*, *Salon*, *The Millions*, and *Newsweek*. As an MFA student, she served as nonfiction editor of Purdue University's literary journal *Sycamore Review*. She teaches at Indiana University-Purdue University Indianapolis, and is the faculty advisor for *genesis*, the literary and art magazine of IUPUI.

Credits

"To the Quick" was first published in *Catapult*. (catapult.co)

"Ophelia Dreams of Sea Urchins" was first published in *Stirring* (stirringlit.com) and later collected in *The Owl was a Baker's Daughter*.

Acknowledgments

The editors would like to thank the following professors and editors for reviewing this textbook in its early stages:

Mark Neely, Professor of English and Editor of *The Broken Plate*, Ball State University

Bill Riley, Assistant Professor of English, Saint Mary of the Woods College

Rachel Hall, Professor of English, SUNY-Geneseo

Kate Watt, Assistant Teaching Professor, University of Missouri-St. Louis

Eleanor Shevlin, Professor of English and Director of Certificate in Publishing, West Chester University

Rachel A. Blumenthal, Assistant Professor of English, Indiana University-Kokomo

P. Andrew Miller, Professor of English, Northern Kentucky University

Amy Barnickel, Lecturer, University of Central Florida

Thom Caraway, Senior English Lecturer, Whitworth University

Kevin McKelvey, Associate Professor of English, University of Indianapolis

Darolyn Jones, Assistant Professor of English, Ball State University

Ann Hostetler, Professor of English, Goshen College

Elizabeth Bobrick, Visiting Scholar, Wesleyan University

Oliver de la Paz, Associate Professor of English, College of the Holy Cross

Brigitte Byrd, Associate Professor of English, Clayton State University

Lindsay Wilson, Community College Professor of English, Truckee Meadows Community College

Ida Stewart, Senior Lecturer, University of the Arts

Christopher Coake, Associate Professor of English, University of Nevada-Reno

Katherine Hoerth, Assistant Professor of English and Editor-in-Chief of LU Literary Press, Lamar University

Sarah Cedeño, Lecturer, English Department, College at Brockport, State University of New York

Heather McPherson, Lecturer, Department of English, Washington University in St. Louis

José Angel Araguz, Ph.D., Assistant Professor, Department of English, Suffolk University

Dinty W. Moore, Founding Editor of *Brevity Magazine* and Professor Emeritus, Ohio University

Janine Harrison, English Instructor, Calumet College of St. Joseph

Key

The edits within this book are designed to mirror those seen on Track Changes in Microsoft Word. To make things clear, edits appear as follows in the book:

~~Struck through text~~ – represents deletions made by editors
<u>Underlined texts</u> – represents suggested insertions by editors
Marginal comments – are comments made by editors

Introduction

Editing is the invisible art. When it's done well, the reader doesn't notice the editor's work, though you can bet the reader will notice a lack of editing. Good editors work behind the scenes, putting writers and their words at center stage. Great editors deliberately avoid the spotlight. (And like stagehands, they look good in black.) But all this invisibility makes editing a hard craft to learn. How can you figure out what you can't see?

Traditionally, the answer has been apprenticeship. If you're lucky, you work under a mentor, picking up their techniques piecemeal. If you're not so lucky, you teach yourself, learning through trial and (lots of) error. Apprentice or autodidact: For years, those have been the only options.

There should be a better way. A more transparent, less haphazard method of learning the craft. That's the aim of this book: to pull back the curtain on the editing process, to make the invisible visible, in order to demystify the editing process.

How this Book is Organized

The layout mirrors the editing process. **Part One** lays the foundation for any editing venture: aesthetic. After helping you discover your aesthetic vision and mission, this part will show you how to communicate it to various audiences.

Part Two moves into the acquisition phase, from solicitation to selection. Here you'll find advice and model texts for corresponding with writers. At the end of the section, two publishers reveal the details of their acquisition process.

Part Three is the heart of this book: case studies in editing. An array of editors have shared real examples of their work, so you'll get to see their editing process in full, from the marked-up manuscript to the final publication. Each case study contains an interview with the editor, in which they talk about their methods and guiding philosophy.

From here, the book moves from observation to application. **Part Four** teaches editing techniques by way of exercises. You can try your hand at editing by applying these techniques in a low-stakes way to one of the stories in the appendix that we lovingly refer to as "CPR dummies."

The Focus of this Book

Here is a rudimentary (but hopefully useful) chart of the editing lifecycle.

Stages of Literary Editing

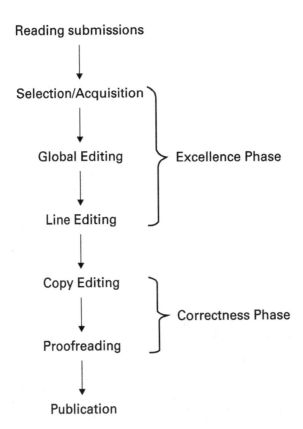

The top half of that chart—the "excellence phase"—is about finding gems and polishing them to reveal their brilliance. In this phase the governing question is *How can I help this story reach its potential?* This book is focused on the excellence phase, and frankly, it's where we find the joy in editing.

The bottom half of the chart is the "correctness phase." These stages are less about elegance and electricity, and more about technical matters: grammar, syntax, continuity. In this phase the governing question is *How do I fix this error?* Make no mistake: this phase is extremely valuable. Copy editors and proofreaders have saved us from looking stupid at least twice in this paragraph alone. This phase is not lesser or lower in any way; it's just not the project of this book.

Likewise, this book won't be dealing with typesetting, publishing, or promotion, although many editors are responsible for these duties, particularly at smaller magazines and presses. Finally, in terms of manuscripts, our focus will be on creative material, by which we mean stories, creative nonfiction essays, poems, memoirs, and novels. While we won't be addressing issues specific to other genres such as journalism or technical writing, the techniques you learn in this book should be applicable to most manuscripts (including ones you've written yourself).

Our goal was to make the ruthlessly practical book we wish someone would have handed to us years ago. Now we're handing it to you.

Good luck. Happy editing. And welcome to the crew.

Bryan Furuness and Sarah Layden

Aesthetic

When we ask our college students to define "aesthetic," their first responses are broad. It's a look, they might say. A mood or a vibe. The feeling or impression you get from seeing both the parts and the whole. How the text and art interact.

Yes, yes, and once again: yes. But that broad base is only the beginning. The aesthetic of literary journals, magazines, and books varies as widely as the individuals who produce them. Trends influence aesthetic, and so does personal taste and sensibility. It's worth paying attention to what you think is good and worthy of admiration. Everyone has likes and dislikes; those are innate responses. But interrogating those responses might reveal deeper, more interesting aspects of your aesthetic: Why do you like what you like? What are the causes and components of that pleasure? How does that translate into the way you edit an essay, a literary magazine, or a novel?

We all have biases, some of which we may need to examine and potentially work against. Are any of our likes or dislikes rooted in a personal experience, causing us to either champion or discount a piece of writing (or a writer)? Are we reading submissions with an open mind, or are we reading through the lens of our preconceptions? Our biases play a role in shaping aesthetic, too.

Editors in the process of developing an aesthetic vision must think about what they want to make, and how to present it to the world. Material and delivery. Content and design. Editors who are conscious of aesthetic are better able to articulate what they're looking for from writers and artists.

Imagine you are creating your own literary publication from scratch. (To get those creative juices flowing, forget about money, time, and other precious resources for a moment.) What will it be? An all-haiku journal? A magazine of first-person essays about nature? Flash fiction, longer stories, entire novellas? Dirty realism, magical realism, high fantasy? Will your publication be online, in print, or both? What shape will it take? (Each issue of *One Story* features a single story, the pages and cover folded and stapled like a 'zine. *HOOT* is a magazine on a postcard.)

As you think about your own aesthetic, seek out and study other models. Think about what you want to make, like a present you give to your readers. A distinctive, singular new thing that is not merely a mood or a feeling, but a special double issue devoted to nostalgia, for example; not just a cool cover, but an image that evokes the Great Depression-era photography of Margaret Bourke-White.

The details are in the discovery.

Mission

If aesthetic speaks to what you want to make, mission is why you want to make it. The purpose of your publication. Its reason for being.

Sounds simple, right? Less slippery than aesthetic, anyway. But as you begin to think about a possible mission, you may find that the line between mission and aesthetic is blurry. If your mission is to be an evangelist for steampunk lit, for example, your answer to "What genre(s) are you open to?" might blur the lines between your aesthetic and your mission.

Our advice: Don't worry about blurring those lines. In art, taste and purpose are often tangled up. It won't be any surprise if they get tangled up in your statements about your publication. The important thing is to craft a clear statement to communicate your publication's identity to your audience. Why is such a statement important? Three reasons, one for each audience for this statement.

1 **For readers**: To inform readers about your reason for existing, and what kind of stuff they might find inside your magazine. Danielle Evans's "Editor's Note" from *American Short Fiction* Issue 72, included later in this chapter, is an excellent example of a reader-focused statement of aesthetic and mission.

2 **For writers**: To attract writers who might submit to your publication, and to attract the kind of submissions you really want. If you're able to clearly articulate your sensibility, it's going to save you time and energy as you read submissions. If you don't tell writers what you want, you'll get all kinds of work that won't be relevant to your sensibility. Wading through your reading queue will become a grind. Clearly articulating your sensibility won't eliminate this problem but should significantly reduce it.

> No matter what, though, you're gonna get porn. Just know that.

3 **For your staff**: A lot of publications have readers on staff who take the first pass on submissions, deciding whether to decline the manuscript or pass it up the editing chain. It will help them (and ultimately you, and your publication) if you provide an aesthetic framework for these decisions. If you don't tell your staff what you want, they'll send along all kinds of stuff that won't be close to your sensibility—and they might end up declining submissions that you would love to read.

> Readers: Staffers whose primary job is to read submissions and make recommendations to editors. Usually, readers are the first eyes on a submission.

Before you articulate your mission and aesthetic vision, it might help to look at a few models. They can easily be found on the "About Us" page on magazine and press sites. You won't search long, though, before you stumble across one that just says, "If you want to get a sense of what we publish, read a few issues." Yes, writers should read the magazines they're submitting to. But a writer can be forgiven for reading a line like this and thinking: *If you want me to spend time and money on your publication, give me a reason. Tell me what I'm in for. Don't make me guess at the menu.*

Maybe you want to be haughty, though. After all, you're in the literary world, the last refuge of haughtiness. But know that saying "read a few issues" will be roundly ignored, and writers will just send you whatever. You will read one misfit submission after another until you plant your Pilot V5 pen into your eye.

Help yourself out. Tell writers what you want. Consider providing a sampling of published work on your site or giving subscribers access to the digital archives. It won't eliminate the problem of misfit submissions but should reduce it.

One final note: Your statement should be an exercise in showing as well as telling. Let your prose exemplify the sensibility and style of your publication. This will attract the kind of readers and writers you want in your orbit.

Example

American Short Fiction Issue 72 Editor's Note (excerpted)
by Danielle Evans | November 24, 2020

I am thrilled to be putting this issue in your hands. It is, as ever, a collection of singular short stories that celebrate the form and highlight its range, but it is also a gift at the end of a turbulent year—work to get lost in, work to be found in, work that in its celebration of emerging writers, and Black emerging writers in particular, encourages us to imagine everything that is yet to come: all of the chances we'll have to see more brilliant work by the writers included here, none of whom yet have a book in print, and all of the chances we'll have to celebrate and center Black writers who have found a way to make room for themselves while we wait for the world to catch up. By definition, an emerging writers issue believes in the future.

Still, when I was invited to guest edit this issue of *American Short Fiction*, I had a brief moment of hesitation. The issue was already in progress, slated as an emerging writers issue, when the editors reached out to me. They had accepted several of the stories included here, and, looking at the accepted work, they wondered how I would feel about coming on board to complete the issue as one focused entirely on emerging Black writers. I thought immediately and excitedly of the writers I'd be thrilled to publish, about how beautiful it would be to put these writers in conversation. I was glad the vision for the issue had come from a place of abundance, not scarcity, from how many talented Black writers were already on our radar and not from a belief that they needed to be searched for. But I also thought, *It is 2020 and we are so tired.*

I worried about the flood of calls for submission Black writers were getting over the summer. It was July—we were grieving the disproportionate impact of the pandemic on our communities and preparing for that grief to continue indefinitely in the absence of a plan or the will to stop it; we were in the streets protesting the latest public police murders, then back in the streets protesting the violence with which the protests were greeted; we were weary, hearing the sinister and familiar language being used to threaten our rights to speech, assembly, due process, and voting; we were weary of the labor it would take to turn the proliferation of expressions of love and support into more than empty gestures. So many of the calls for work by Black writers going out last summer were calls to respond immediately to recent events, as though any of us could adequately respond in real time to what hadn't finished happening yet, as though many of us hadn't already been writing work about what was happening all along, work that provided the kind of context the market now said it wanted, only to have that work ignored or dismissed. A part of me felt like I had no business asking anyone for art when what we needed was the safety of a space to rest.

But of course, believing that Black Lives Matter means more than setting the bar at basic survival—it means investing in space for Black people to thrive, investing in space that feels celebratory and liberatory and provides our work the freedom to name its terms. When I said yes, in spite of my moment of hesitation, it was because I envisioned an issue exactly like this one. In this issue are nine stories from writers at the beginning of extraordinary careers.

One of the writers in these pages is being published for the very first time. Two have books scheduled to be published next year. Others have collected impressive credentials, including the Plimpton Prize and an appearance in *The Best American Short Stories*. All of these writers are people whom, if we're lucky, we'll be reading for a very long time. I am wary when, in times of trouble, people declare that we've lived through worse and will live through this. Not all of us did and not all of us will. But reading work like this reminds me that there will be a future and that future will be more than the grief we carry into it. If sometimes our present joy is like the joy in Lucille Clifton's "won't you celebrate with me," the joy that *every day, something has tried to kill me and has failed*, well then we'll take it, and we'll celebrate.

Danielle Evans is the author of the story collections *The Office of Historical Corrections* and *Before You Suffocate Your Own Fool Self*. Her work has won awards and honors including the PEN American Robert W. Bingham Prize, the Hurston-Wright award for fiction, and a National Endowment for the Arts fellowship. Her stories have appeared in magazines including *The Paris Review*, *A Public Space*, *American Short Fiction*, *Callaloo*, *The Sewanee Review*, and *Phoebe*, and have been anthologized in *The Best American Short Stories* and *New Stories from the South*. She teaches in The Writing Seminars at Johns Hopkins University.

Practice

Goal: To discover and express your own sensibility and sense of mission.

To Consider

Let's say you're running a magazine or a press. How will you describe what you want to publish? Why does your publication exist—and why should readers care? Here are some prompts to help you think through your mission and aesthetic vision.

Maybe you are! But even if you're not (yet) producing a publication, take a swing at this exercise. Think of it as practice for the day you're running your own publishing empire.

Sensibility

What genre(s) are you open to?

Are there any topics you'd like to publish (or any topics you don't want to see)--and why?

How would you describe an ideal submission for your publication? What are its salient features and characteristics?

What makes a submission good? What do you value in a submission?

Where does your sensibility fit in the literary tradition? How might it be categorized?

What literary traditions does your publication uphold? What traditions does it challenge?

Who are some writers (or what are some books, or stories, or songs, or statues, or whatever) that perfectly embody your sensibility?

What magazines are like yours? What magazines do you emulate?

How would you describe your publication in one line?

Reason for Being

Are there certain types of manuscripts or writers you'd like to publish (or any types that you don't want to publish)—and why?

Why should the rest of us be reading this work? What can it do for us? How would it affect our lives?

Why should your publication exist? Why does it matter?

If we took a flamethrower to every one of your publications, past and present and future, what would any of us lose? Why should anyone care?

Esoterica

Describe your ideal reader. What kind of shoes do they wear? What music do they listen to?

What are the ideal circumstances in which to experience your publication?

What drink pairs well with your publication?

Fill in the blanks:

If you like_____, you'll love this publication.

If you could eat my publication, it would taste like_____, and it would leave you_____.

To Do: Build a Prototype Journal

Goal: To discover and express your design aesthetic.

Deciding what to publish is only part of your aesthetic vision. Your decisions about what form it will take (i.e. design) is the other part. With this exercise, you'll try your hand at publication design.

Here's the job: Design a literary journal that represents a mission and aesthetic of your choosing. Scout out models online, at the bookstore, and the library, noting what's been done before and considering what you'd like to accomplish. Get hands-on with paper, scissors, glue, and collage materials from other magazines; see what inspires. If you decide that your magazine will appear in print, create a mock-up version that includes an originally designed, representative cover. If you decide that your magazine will be exclusively online, create a detailed mock-up of the home page. These mock-ups can be digital or analog, your choice.

Acquisition
From Attraction to Acceptance, from Solicitation to Slush

Acquisition > Editing > Publication

No matter how big or small your literary enterprise, the editing process starts with submissions, the manuscripts you receive from writers. As *Barrelhouse* puts it, "submissions are the fossil fuel that keeps the Barrelhouse moped puttering along the side of the literary highway."

Broadly speaking, there are two types of submissions: solicited and unsolicited.

Solicited Submissions

Think of a solicitation as a personal invitation. You reach out to a writer whose work you admire and ask them to submit a manuscript. The typical solicitation promises careful consideration, not publication. (Promising to publish work you have not seen will eventually lead to editor's regret. Even the best writers can write some godawful stuff.)

When writing a solicitation, be clear about what you're offering, and be careful not to overpromise. Here's a model:

Dear Mr. O'Nan,

My name is Zora Watson. I'm the editor of *Warp & Weft*, and a big fan of your work. *Night Country* is one of my favorite books. It's gripping and suspenseful and lyrical all at once, and because the characters feel so real, the story is all the more terrifying.

Why bother telling the author what you admire about their work?
(a) So your claim of "being a big fan" doesn't come off as bullshit.
(b) To show yourself to be a smart reader who understands their project, which implies that you just might be a good editor for their work.
(c) Because buttering up a writer is never a bad idea, especially before asking them for something. (If this makes you feel skeevy or manipulative, keep in mind that we're not asking you to say anything you don't actually mean. After all, you're soliciting this writer because you love their work, right?) At its core, this letter is a persuasive essay. You're making the case for this writer to trust you with their work.

Include a call to action.

This is the kind of writing we love to feature in *Warp & Weft*—which brings me to the reason I'm reaching out to you today. Would you send us some of your work? We'd love to read a story, or an essay, or an opening chapter of a new novel. While I can't promise publication sight unseen, of course, I can promise careful and generous consideration.

1. Specific directions are helpful.
2. Often, letting the writer bypass your standard submission portal makes them feel extra-special, like some kind of dignitary. Why bother? See the earlier note about how this solicitation is a persuasive essay. However, if this special treatment offends your populist sensibilities, you could tell the writer to submit their manuscript through the normal channels and that you'll keep an eye out for their submission.

You can send your submission directly to me at editor@warpandweft.com. Thank you for your consideration!

This model, like all the models in this book, is meant to be malleable and generative. You are welcome to adjust it to your voice and needs, or to discard it entirely and come up with something better. A model should be a springboard, not a prison.

One more note about solicitation: It doesn't always work out. Sarah once edited for a magazine that solicited a soon-to-be famous writer; he politely declined to submit because he had a first-look contract with *The New Yorker*. Bryan worked for a magazine that started off soliciting big-name writers for the first couple of issues, but ended up declining most of their submissions.

Rejecting a solicited piece can be awkward for everyone, but if you do it with grace, most writers will take it well. The key is to be as personal and warm in the rejection as you were in the solicitation. If you change your tone—if you go from a personal solicitation to a form rejection (which will be covered in detail later in this book)—the writer may feel shunned. To avoid hurt feelings and the attendant drama, consider the following model for rejecting a solicited piece:

You solicited the story. You don't owe her publication, but you owe her an explanation of why the piece doesn't work for you. Give evidence of the careful consideration that you promised.

Dear Ms. Shanning,

Thank you for submitting your story, "The Soldier, the Devil, and the Violin" to *Warp & Weft*. We loved the characters, but our readers were confused by the ending, which felt abrupt. While we're going to take a pass on this story,

End on a positive note and keep the door open.

we remain fans of your work. Please consider sending us another story in the future.

Practice

To Do

Write a solicitation to a writer you admire. Feel free to reference the model texts above.

Unsolicited Submissions

If a writer sends you work without a personal invitation, it's considered unsolicited. For most publications, this category accounts for the vast majority of submissions. Though, if you think about it, is any work truly "unsolicited?" The mere act of declaring your publication open for submissions is an act of solicitation. Also, magazines and presses are always posting general calls for submissions in mags like *Poets & Writers* and the *AWP Chronicle*, and on sites like Duotrope and NewPages, and what are these calls but blanket solicitations?

The term "unsolicited" might be a misnomer, but since everyone uses it, we're stuck with it, just like we're stuck with its gross synonym "slush." If you hear an editor refer to "the slush pile," they're talking about the mass of unsolicited submissions awaiting their attention.

Submission Guidelines

With your mission and vision statement, you've told writers what you want to publish. Your submission guidelines will tell writers how to send their manuscripts to you.

When it comes to submission guidelines, clarity is king. If your guidelines are vague or confusing, your job will be much harder in the most mundane ways. Your inbox will brim over with emails requesting clarification. Submissions will pour in the wrong channels and end up in the wrong places. And when you lose track of a manuscript that came in the wrong way, the writer will slag you on social media, and you will be so angry you'll burst a blood vessel in your eye and literally see red, which, frankly, you thought was just a saying.

Editors, allow us to offer an ounce of prevention. Clear guidelines that anticipate likely areas of confusion will go a long way toward creating an orderly system that will allow you to spend more of your time reading and editing, and less of your time chasing and clarifying.

How do you craft clear guidelines? What should you include? Good questions. Get thee to Google for some answers. For this exercise (and the next few, as well), your first step will be research.

Practice

Goal: To communicate your technical guidelines and submission process to writers.

To Consider

Find and read five submission guidelines online. Then answer the following questions:

Where are they found?
How do they tend to be structured? What components do they include?
What are the conventions and characteristics of this form?
What questions do they answer?
What problems or objections do they anticipate?
What tone do they strike?
How do they set the submitter's expectations for a response?
What makes a good one?
What makes a bad one?

On the whole, how could these guidelines be better?

What do you know now that you didn't know before you started this exercise—about the publishing world, or about yourself? What are you learning about the kind of editor you are?

Regarding submission guidelines in general, what questions do you have? What do you still want to know?

To Do

> For this one, you might do a little research into web content accessibility.

Write your own submission guidelines. Make sure they jibe with your mission and aesthetic vision statement. All your communiqués should fit together; they should all arise from the same sensibility and strike a similar tone. As you write, consider how you might anticipate:

- A writer who is visually impaired
- A writer who is without internet access (and cannot get to a library)
- A wildly arrogant writer. For this one, ask yourself: If I were such a writer, how could I screw up this system and annoy the editor? How might the editor guard against these problems, or outline consequences for such fuckery?

Call for Submissions

Submission guidelines are important, but this document is usually "homebound" on your publication's website. Such a document depends on writers coming to it—but how will you summon those writers?

A good step is to put together a "call for submissions," an invitation posted on various literary sites for writers to send you manuscripts. The trick is to craft the call for submissions in a way that will do some pre-sorting for you, attracting the kind of submissions you want to read and gently repelling the stuff you don't want.

Practice

Goal: To elicit the kind of submissions you want to receive.

To Consider

Search online for a bunch of calls for submissions. Find out what other publications are doing in this regard and how they're doing it. These calls should be easy to find (in fact, that's one sign of a good call). A minute of googling will turn up thousands.

Pick 7-10 calls and study them. Take notes on the following questions:

- Where are they found? (Which is another way of asking: Where could your publication list its call?)
- What are the conventions of this form?

- What components are essential to a good call?
- What makes a good call good?
- What makes a bad call bad?
- What are the essential components of a good call?
- How specific should a call be? Is there a risk to making it too specific?

To Do

Apply what you've learned to write your own call for submissions. While a good call often contains elements of a mission & aesthetic vision statement along with components of submission guidelines, it's usually a good deal shorter than either of those pieces. You might think of this activity as an exercise in dilation. How can you capture the essence and tone of those other documents in a shorter form?

Strategies for Dealing with Submissions

Let's say you've put out the call and submissions are rolling in by the truckload. How do you deal with them?

Stage 1: First Cull

Because most magazines receive far more submissions than they can ever hope to publish (or even discuss as a whole staff), the first step is winnowing. What submissions can be eliminated right away? Some magazines leave this task to their front-line readers. Other magazines ask their section editors—the Fiction Editor, the Poetry Editor, etc.—to make the first read and cull the weak submissions before passing the stronger submissions to their readers. At the lit mag *Agni*, the first cull is made by the Editor-in-Chief, Sven Birkerts.

In an editor's note on the *Agni* site, Birkerts writes about his approach by telling the story of an ordinary morning. As you'll see, the note was written before the journal started using an online submission tool. "I drive, I park (bear with me), I make my way across the [Boston University] campus to the building at 236 Bay State Road. My first stop is the fourth floor, where I nearly always find a mountain of mail, which I load into a plastic postal container and carry down to our second-floor office." After separating the mail into piles according to genre, he's left with a stack of prose submissions "that is often a foot high."

Next comes the part that might shock you if you haven't worked at a magazine. "Over the next hour or so," Birkerts writes, "I will have worked through that whole stack, delegating all but a handful of submissions to the return (read: rejection) bin. The survivors get rubber-banded and passed along to my largely volunteer readers."

Spending a single hour on a thousand manuscript pages might seem cruel to you, but it's merely practical. Editors simply don't have the time to read every page of every submission. The first stage has to be triage. At most magazines, an initial reader will scan the first page or two of a submission to see if the writer will give him a reason to cast it away.

"As an editor I need to be able to tell quickly," writes Birkerts in "Screening the Essay" on *Essay Daily*. "Time is in short supply, and submissions throng the sluices like salmon in spawning season. Yes, the editor needs to know exactly what he's looking for, and he needs to be cruel—which is to say he needs to believe in his taste."

Beware of other cruelty in your practice, though. It's easy to become jaded in this business. Easy to get so overwhelmed with submissions that you start to resent them. Easy for the tiniest bit of gatekeeping authority to trigger an inflated sense of your own importance.

If that happens, remember that writers have made themselves vulnerable by submitting to you—"submission" has multiple meanings, after all—and consider how you should respond in kind. Consider how you'd want to be treated—and how you'd want your submission to be treated—as a submitter.

Think about what kind of editor you want to be. And if the answer is *A dictator!*, it might be time for you to get out of the business.

Stage 2: Deeper Consideration

Submissions that survive the initial cull are usually sent to a small band of readers, who are tasked with reading each piece fully and carefully. In this age of online submission databases, the readers generally make notes about their response, and often cast a vote of *yes*, *no*, or *maybe* on each submission.

Eventually the editors of each section—Fiction, Poetry, Nonfiction, etcetera—make another cull, deciding which pieces will move on to all-staff discussion, and which pieces will be rejected.

Stage 3: All-Staff Discussion

In the first stage, each submission had a single reader who decided whether to reject or advance the piece. In the next stage, each submission had a handful of readers. For this final stage, each submission is read and discussed by the entire staff. As you can see, the movement is toward fewer pieces having more readers and deeper consideration.

If you've ever had the chance to work on a lit mag or a press, most of your memories are probably from the all-staff discussions. Remember the time that a submission had a single advocate, and through careful and passionate persuasion, that reader got everybody else to see the beauty of the piece? It was like *Twelve Angry Men* in real life! Or that time when everybody loved that stupid story except for you and you felt like the kid yelling, "The Emperor has no clothes!" only no one believed you?

Sometimes you'll leave an all-staff discussion trembling with exhilaration; sometimes you'll leave shaking your head at the group's idiocy. The stakes are high for each submission—they've come a long way, and at the end of this night they'll either be crowned or killed—but at all-staff discussions, it feels like the stakes are high for you, too.

Because they are. Your job is important. Writers and readers everywhere are depending on you.

Different publications have different strategies for dealing with submissions, of course. What we mapped out here is just one general model, so general in fact that we can't think of a single publication that doesn't depart from it in some way. To complement the general, we offer the particular. Below are two actual depictions of acquisition: one from a literary magazine and one from a press.

Spotlight: *descant* Literary Magazine

Matthew Pitt, Editor of *descant*

On Logistics

Since I began my tenure as Editor, *descant* has been fortunate to have a graduate student's assistance during our academic year. Initially, this graduate assistant logged each fiction and poetry submission on an Excel spreadsheet—regardless if it came in via USPS or our Submittable online option. At this point, we accept work only through Submittable, with two key exceptions: if the writer does not have Internet access, and/or if the writer is incarcerated. On occasion, if I see a submission from a writer whose work I admire, or one who came very close to acceptance with a prior submission, I will ask the assistant to assign it directly to me straightaway. Otherwise, the graduate assistant assigns submissions to an appropriate Associate Editor within the genre. Submissions are divided equally among this group of readers, so no one editor (hopefully) is too burdened. Submissions are also distributed democratically: in other words, one editor wouldn't receive only work from newer writers, while another receives only work from writers with significant publication credits.

When a short story or poetry submission receives a positive reading from an Associate Editor, the piece moves on to the second stage. On the poetry side, promising submissions are passed up to our Poetry Editor. On the fiction side, promising submissions are forwarded to my attention after receiving a first read. If these pieces come to us via Submittable, the editor can vote his or her preference with a simple click (yea, nay, or maybe). These submissions also often include a brief note from the Associate Fiction Editor who read it first, describing the story's virtues, and identifying a few questions or concerns. I tend to not read these notes until I've given the work a read. Once I have, though, it provides terrific context, which may affirm my reading, or suggest some aspect of the story I hadn't fully considered. In both instances, it transforms the action from just pushing paper from one party to the next, into the realm of a true editorial conversation.

Since *descant* is an annual publication, the editors have time to mull over intriguing submissions for a spell. Many submissions produce a visceral, immediate reaction (sometimes good, sometimes ill). Some are more problematic, though, which could suggest craft issues that aren't yet harmonious. It could also suggest that the story in question has functioned like a time-release capsule, taking a little longer to enter the editor's bloodstream, but lingering once it's there. In the end, the Poetry Editor makes publication decisions on the poetry side, and I make the final decisions on the fiction side.

On Equity

VIDA is a "feminist literary organization . . . dedicated to creating transparency surrounding gender imbalances and the lack of diversity in the literary landscape." With their annual count, VIDA provides a snapshot of the current gender breakdown in literary journals. To learn more, see vidaweb.org

When I started as Editor, the gender disparity in our total tally of submissions was stark. I had read troubling statistics noting how women often stopped sending their writing to journals if the initial submissions weren't accepted. Once the VIDA Count came on my radar, seeing the stark gender imbalance in so many publications dispirited me, but also served as a call to action. With all this in mind, I endeavored to offer encouraging notes to women whose work the staff admired, even if we ultimately declined it. By citing specifics, I hoped to send a strong signal that their voices had affected us, set a conversation in motion, one we hoped would be ongoing. And it has produced real effects: submission numbers are far more balanced in terms of gender, and I know many occasions where such writers kept trying us, until a submission chimed perfectly.

This back-and-forth between staff and contributors has amplified underrepresented voices in our pages, in general. As a result, the journal is engaging in broader, deeper conversations. It makes for more stirring issues! There is real reading rhapsody in having your worldview expanded by encountering critical voices outside the realm of your experience, that too often go unheard.

While the pandemic led to budgetary constrictions—and costs of Submittable accounts have increased—we fortunately have not yet had to implement a reading fee. Fee-free submissions ensure there is no financial barrier precluding writers from sharing their voices. At the same time, incarcerated writers—whose Internet access is limited—can continue sending work via USPS. Each of our last few editions includes work from incarcerated writers. As a resident of the state operating the country's largest prison system, I find this personally and profoundly important. These, too, are voices that often go unheard.

Spotlight: Rose Metal Press

Abigail Beckel and Kathleen Rooney | Cofounders, Rose Metal Press

Rose Metal Press, a mission-driven nonprofit literary publisher, releases two full-length titles per year in hybrid literary genres, which we define expansively to include flash fiction and nonfiction, prose poetry, book-length lyric essays, image-and-text work, collaborations, and any other project that stands with a foot in more than one traditional genre's territory. We are particularly interested in writing that takes a fully hybrid form: recently we have published or acquired books that are organized as an abecedarian, a poetic encyclopedia, and brief prose pieces based on each word from a Shakespeare sonnet.

For these full-length books, we have two separate acquisition processes. If we are looking for an anthology, like our *Field Guides to Writing Flash Fiction, Prose Poetry*, or *Flash Nonfiction*, or our hybrid genre craft guide *Family Resemblance*, or our *Field Guide to Graphic Literature: Artists and Writers on Creating Graphic Narratives, Poetry Comics, and Literary Collage*, we typically start by having a call for anthology pitches from the potential editors and choose from a number of comprehensive pitches. The editors write up their plan for assembling the book and a list of authors they think ought to be included and, once we select an anthology concept to pursue, we help the editors shape that list for diversity in every aspect from aesthetic approach to racial and gender inclusivity. We also help guide the book's structure and assist in soliciting the contributing authors for original work and essays. We've also occasionally received and accepted pitches for anthologies outside of our official reading periods.

When we are looking for full-length books that are not anthologies (the majority of our list), we acquire new projects by way of open reading periods that we hold periodically, usually every other spring/summer. Sometimes the open reading periods are for hybrid work in general, where we consider any projects the author(s) identify as hybrid. Once again, hybrid for us means the combining of two literary forms to create a new form of expression. Other times, we narrow the parameters of the reading period down to a type of hybrid work we are particularly seeking for our list at a given point, such as issuing a call for image-and-text work, or prose poetry, or linked flash collections.

For our open reading periods, we ask authors to submit using Submittable, but we don't require the manuscripts to be anonymous and we read them with knowledge of the authors' identities. We love open reading periods because they give us a chance to discover new voices—new to us and often new to the literary scene—and see what kind of hybrid work the wider field of writers is doing. For this reason, we rarely solicit work, preferring instead to consider finished manuscripts during open reading periods. We usually choose two to four manuscripts to publish from each reading period, generally out of a field of several hundred projects. During these open reading periods, we are looking for the best and most innovative work in a wide range of styles and voices.

As noted above, manuscripts submitted to our open reading periods (or pitches submitted for anthologies) are not read anonymously. For our annual Short Short Chapbook Contest, which we held for twelve years and which ended in 2018, the manuscripts were considered anonymously by an outside judge—someone well known in the flash field—but we're not sure we'd use that format again. What at that time seemed like the fairest way to judge manuscripts, we have come to realize (like many other presses), is not necessarily the most fair or inclusive way since taste is so subjective. Most small presses or imprints have a stylistic aesthetic that is recognizable. But it's important not to confuse aesthetics with unconscious bias toward certain themes, identities, or voices. A manuscript feels like a Rose Metal Press book not because of who wrote it but because of the ways it innovates and surprises us with its form and story. Our open reading periods allow us to build our list out for several years ahead, so we value knowing who the people that have sent their work in are, and making sure that the manuscripts we select and the RMP catalog we develop reflect a multitude of creative approaches and personal identities. Not reading anonymously also allows us to know the make-up (age, race, gender, and so forth) of our submitters, which then allows us to do more outreach as needed to communities that are underrepresented to solicit submissions. In short, knowing who our submitters are and where they are coming from helps counter potential bias and allows us to read more deliberately and with an eye toward selecting for the most variety—on every level, but especially diversity, equity, and inclusion—as possible.

To cite a recent example, during our most recent open reading period in 2020, we were able to offer waived submission fees to BIPOC writers, which assisted a great deal in diversifying our submissions. The no-fee option encouraged and allowed more writers of color to submit manuscripts, enriching the entire process as a result and broadening the range of voices and stories we could highlight through book publication.

We generally do not read pitches or manuscripts outside of our designated reading periods. These breaks from the acquisition process give us the needed time to focus on the books we have acquired and give them the editorial, design, and marketing attention they deserve. We know there is tons of great hybrid writing out there, and often have to say no to many interesting and worthy projects simply due to lack of space in our relatively small list and our desire to carefully hone and enthusiastically promote each book we do get the privilege to publish.

Responding to Submissions

Every submission requires a response. Your options might seem binary—either it's accepted or rejected, right?—but actually there are different types of acceptances and rejections. Imagine a spectrum, ranging from unconditional acceptance to a form rejection with many points in between. Following are a few models from the most common points on that spectrum, moving from the positive end to the negative end.

Unconditional Acceptance

You want the story. You think it's stellar. A part of you will die if you do not get it. At some point you may ask to take an editing pass at the story, but publication is not contingent upon editing.

Model

Dear <Author Name>,

Thank you for submitting "Denny Comes Back" to *Little Offices*. We love it, and we want to publish it in our next issue. At your earliest convenience, would you let us know if it's still available?

> Why this question? Because most writers send their submission to multiple magazines at once (in a widely-accepted practice called "simultaneous submission.") If the submission is accepted at one place, the writer is supposed to withdraw it from consideration at all the other magazines but sometimes they forget to do so. This question is a way of making sure that the manuscript hasn't already been accepted elsewhere.

Conditional Acceptance

The story is powerful, but not fully realized. You think you can get it to that point, though, if the writer will work with you.

Model

Dear <Author Name>,

Thank you for submitting "Denny Comes Back" to *The Lonesome Oak Review*. We love <insert specifics here>, but some of our readers got hung up on <a specific issue or two>. Bottom line: We like this piece a lot, but we think it has the potential to be even stronger with another draft. We will commit to publishing that next draft if you're willing to work with one of our editors who, by the way, is a big advocate for your story. Would you be open to that process?

> "If" is the key word in this letter.

Specific Conditional Acceptance

You like the submission, except for one element that's a dealbreaker. If the writer agrees to change that element, though, you'll take the piece.

Model

Dear <Author Name>,

Thank you for submitting "Denny Comes Back" to *Limberlost*. There's so much to admire about this piece, from <specific detail> to <specific detail>, but I was thrown by the ending when Denny turns into a coyote, particularly because there were no other magical or supernatural elements in the story. Furthermore, the move allows Denny to slip away from taking responsibility for the mess that he's made. To my mind, keeping him human and making him live with his mess would make a more powerful and compelling ending.

The rest of the piece is great, though. If you'd be willing to revisit the ending (and let Denny stay human), I'd love to publish it. If you feel like this suggestion harms the story, though, we'll part ways and I'll wish you the best of luck in finding another home for this piece. If we can't come to terms on this project, we'd love to see another submission from you in the future.

> Specific deadlines can be useful to both parties, as they set clear expectations.

Thanks for your consideration. If you can let us know your answer by Monday, December 11th, I'd appreciate it.

Invitation to Revise and Resubmit

You like a lot about the piece, but it's not close enough to achieving its potential to warrant a conditional acceptance. Still, you don't want to let it go entirely. You can give some suggestions and let the writer know you'd be willing to read another draft.

Model

Dear <Author Name>,

Thank you for submitting "East Chicago, Winter, 1997" to *Stir*. I found so much to like about your piece, especially the final image of the father lying face-down in the puddle, but the beginning was confusing. In the first three pages, we're introduced to eight characters, five locations, and two time-frames—most of which don't seem integral to the events and the image at the end of the story.

While I can't publish the story in its current form, I'd be willing to read another draft if you can streamline the story's opening. If you take me up on this invitation, just email the new draft to me directly. If you'd rather pass, I'll wish you the best of luck placing this story elsewhere and invite you to submit other work to us in the future.

Personalized Rejection

This submission was close. Not close enough for an invitation to resubmit, but strong enough that you want to offer a little feedback and encouragement.

Model

Dear <Author Name>,

Thank you for submitting "Tooth and Claw" to *Horace: The Mag*. While we appreciated your attention to sensory detail, our readers wanted more dramatic tension, particularly in the beginning. We're going to take a pass on this piece, but we'd love to see more work from you in the future.

> You may have noticed that this letter uses "we" instead of "I." We want to show you some options. For your own responses, you can use first-person or the "editorial we." Your call.

As a point of pride and literary service, some publications commit to personalizing all rejections. Other magazines will not send any personalized rejections because (a) it invests time and energy in stuff they're not going to publish, and (b) some writers will react to the personalized response in unpleasant ways (See the end of this chapter for more on this nonsense and how to deal with it). Many magazines split the difference and send out personalized rejections on about 10–20 percent of submissions.

Warm Form Rejection

AKA "Encouraging" Rejection

You're not taking this story, but you see promise here. The writer's next story (or maybe the one after that) might be the right fit for your magazine.

Model

Dear <Author Name>,

Thank you for submitting to *Snake Dancer*. While this piece isn't quite right for us, we enjoyed your writing. Please send us more work in the future. Best of luck in placing this submission elsewhere.

Form Rejection

For most magazines, the form rejection is used for the vast majority of submissions. Be clear and brief. Rip that bandage off quickly.

Model

Dear <Author Name>,

Thank you for submitting to **Goo**. We appreciate the chance to read your work. After careful consideration, the editorial staff has decided that we are not the right market for this piece. Best of luck elsewhere.

Best Practices in Rejection

We especially love it when a big publication warns a writer against simultaneous submission and refuses to tell you when you're rejected. Your story might be out of the running on day one, but they want you to sit around for three months before submitting it somewhere else, like a period of mourning. The arrogance!

1. **Actually send rejections**

This might seem like a no-brainer, but some magazines have a weird habit of *not* sending out rejections. This practice used to be exclusive to the biggest publications, your *New Yorker*s and *Atlantic*s, who at least owned up to the policy in their submission guidelines by saying something like *If you haven't heard from us in three months, you'll know we're not interested.* Even so, it's snooty and demeaning, right? They're basically saying they're too important to acknowledge you.

More recently, some smaller mags have adopted a similar policy of passive rejections. Most of these magazines use an online submission tool like Submittable, and they'll change a submission's status to "declined," but they won't send the writer a message. The writer has to find out on their own by logging onto Submittable. Learning about rejection this way feels like coming out of the bathroom to discover that your date has snuck out of the restaurant.

We don't think the editors of these smaller magazines are being snooty. We also don't think they're lazy (with online submission tools, sending out a form rejection takes no more time or thought than changing the status of a piece to "declined"). They're probably doing it because it's uncomfortable to tell someone no.

You know what else is uncomfortable? Submitting a manuscript to a publication. By offering their work up for judgment, the writer has taken a risk. Respect that risk, editors. Reciprocate. Keep the scales in balance.

2. Respond in a timely fashion

Admittedly, "timely" is a fuzzy term, and open to interpretation. But you should define what "timely" means for your publication by including your response time in your submission guidelines, even if it's phrased in an aspirational way (e.g. *We strive to respond to submissions in four to six weeks.*).

As writers, Sarah and Bryan have submitted stories to magazines that have taken over a year to respond. "Timely" is a fuzzy term, but not that damn fuzzy. If your publication is taking that long, it's time to reconsider your approach. You're not treating writers fairly.

3. Admit when you screw up

Post your response time and do your best to live up to it. But if something happens to put you behind, fess up. Most writers will be understanding and supportive.

4. Don't bullshit writers in your rejection

The phrase *Your submission is not right for us at this time* shows up in a surprising number of rejections. It begs the question: When would it be right for you? Unless you want writers to resubmit the same piece every six months, drop this cliché from your rejection.

The same goes for mentions of space. *We don't have space for your story in our issue.* That is not why you're rejecting the piece, editors. You're rejecting it because you don't think it's good enough, or because it doesn't fit your mission or aesthetic vision. You don't have to come out and say that directly—*We are not going to publish your story on account of we hate it*—but don't blame other factors. You don't want to see bullshit in the submissions, so don't bullshit in your rejection. Be respectful, but be forthright.

5. Rejection and sales should not be bedfellows

Subscriptions. Editing services. Enrollment in overseas retreats. All kinds of sales pitches accompany rejections, and it's all bad form. It's also bad timing. When someone gets rejected, they're not in a mood to buy anything but Häagen-Dazs and Wild Turkey.

Actually, some people *will* buy the stuff you package up with rejection. Your pairing might give some submitters the erroneous idea of a *quid pro quo: If I buy this thing, I might stand a better chance of publishing here in the future.* For other submitters, the rejection has beaten down their defenses and your offer finds them in a low and vulnerable state. Congratulations: You've negged a few sad souls into a $6 subscription. Can you really feel good about that?

Decouple sales from rejection. Hit up your potential subscribers/students/retreat attendees at a different time in a different way. It'll be better for both of you.

Dealing with Blowback

Sometimes writers will respond to your rejection. This is rarely pleasant. At best it smacks of strained positivity (*Thanks so much!!! I will use this to try even harder and do better next time!!!!!*) but usually it's bitter. Here are a few common types that you can expect.

The angry dude: Yes, this type is always a dude. He usually comes back at you with something like *I knew you didn't have the guts to publish something this edgy* or *Whew! I regretted my decision to submit to your dumb mag. Thanks for letting me off the hook!*

Other times, the angry dude responds to your personalized rejection by arguing the point. *Dear "Editor": The ending was intentionally abrupt because that's the way life ends: abruptly.*

It probably won't surprise you to learn that this type of blowback happens more frequently to editors who identify as female.

The request for feedback: Some writers will respond to a rejection with a request. *Can you tell me more about what didn't work, exactly? I'm totally open to feedback!*

The Just-So-You-Know: The previous types of responses in this list tend to come on the heels of a rejection. The Just-So-You-Know usually arrives a few weeks or months after your rejection in the form of a note from the writer saying, *Hi there. I just wanted to give you a heads-up that the piece you rejected has been picked up by the* Tuskwart Review. *Just thought you might want to know!*

> The best part is the light, chipper tone, like a spritz of Pine-sol in a porta-potty.

The subtext, of course, is *See how you blew it?* The writer wants you to feel bad.

You probably shouldn't. Different publications have different sensibilities. Not every quality piece is a good fit for every publication. What works for *Tuskwart* may not work for you. Somebody else accepting a piece you have rejected doesn't mean you're doing something wrong; it's simply the way publishing works.

So how should you deal with blowback? We have two suggestions.

1. **Don't**

There is no way to win. The complaining writer will not suddenly transform into a reasonable person and admit that you make a good point. Your time is limited and valuable; don't spend it wrestling with trolls. To paraphrase Lieutenant Anita Van Buren from *Law & Order*, "Don't take the bait, and don't escalate."

One exception to this recommendation: the writers asking for more feedback are almost always new to the publishing world. Their intentions are good; they just don't know how to play the game yet, and they are unaware of all the demands on an editor's time. Let these writers down easy. You might design a prefabricated message that goes something like: *I wish we could offer more feedback, but given the volume of submissions, it's simply impossible.*

2. **Build a firewall**

Send rejections from your magazine's address, not your personal one. If you want an even thicker firewall, you can sign the rejection with THE EDITORS instead of your name (though we're torn on this. On one hand, it's important to take responsibility for a rejection. On the other hand, once you've caught flak from one too many angry dudes, no one's going to blame you if you remove your name from the rejection slip.).

Practice

To Do

Read a story (either a CPR Dummy story in the appendix or, if you're making a magazine, a submission to your publication). Write three different responses to the writer. Each response should come from a different point on the response spectrum (e.g. acceptance, conditional acceptance, invitation to revise and resubmit, etc.). The voice of your responses should fit the sensibility of your publication. For instance, if your magazine is supposed to be punk rock in paper form, your form rejection probably shouldn't be like: *My dearest Mr. Roxroth: We regret to inform you, etc.*

Correspondence

Recently we heard about a poet who was upset with her editor. One of her poems used the numeral 9, and the editor wanted her to change it to "nine." The poet was complaining to her writer friends, asking them if she should write an angry letter to the editor, or pull the manuscript from the magazine.

We have a guess about what led to this mess. The editor probably sent the poet suggestions without any rationale for the change, and without guidance about how the poet could respond. The change from "9" to "nine" might have been a suggestion, but the writer was taking it as a directive.

The point is this: Marking on a manuscript is only half the game. Communicating with writers—setting expectations, explaining your rationale, laying out timelines—is the other half of the game, and it is just as important. You can make the best suggestions, but if you bungle your communication, your writers will end up confused or irritated.

Remember, you're not just working on a manuscript. You're working with a writer on a manuscript. Editing is a three-legged race. If you don't want to get dragged through the dirt, communication and coordination with the writer is key.

In this chapter we'll cover several types of communication, starting with the initial contact following acquisition. Sometimes this communication happens over the phone or in person, but usually it is conducted through written correspondence.

Initial Contact

The manuscript has been acquired. Time to contact the writer and start the editing process. In your initial contact, you'll want to introduce yourself, your publication, and your purpose for contacting the writer.

It's also a good idea to lay out the "rules of the game." Give the whole timeline, from when you'll send the edits to the publication date. Let the writer know how to respond to your marks and comments. A common practice is to say that your edits are suggestions, and that the writer can take what makes sense and disregard the rest. Typically, the writer has final say over the manuscript, especially if you have already agreed in the acquisition phase to publish it.

You may also consider telling the writer what kind of editor you are. Bryan has a heavy hand, but he welcomes pushback from the writer. That's how he knows the editor and writer are both deeply engaged with the story. Bryan finds it helpful to let the writer know about his style early on, so the writer is not overwhelmed and pissed/depressed when they receive their marked-up manuscript in the next stage. Sarah, who has been edited by Bryan, can attest to all of the above. She approaches editing with a somewhat lighter touch, showing the writer where clarification and refining are needed.

Finally, end every message to the writer with a note about the next steps and timeline. What comes next, and when?

Model

Dear Helen,

Roy Barnes here, editor for *The Glass Harp*. I love your essay, "Shade Tree," and I'm excited to edit it with you. For a pub date, we're looking at May 1, which means we'll need to get the final manuscript to the copywriter by April 20th at the latest. To allow time for the possibility of multiple rounds of editing, I'll send my suggestions and the marked-up manuscript by this weekend.

FYI: I'm a pretty hands-on editor, especially when I'm really engaged by a manuscript. But I am open to pushback from writers, and in the end, it's your piece, and you'll get to make the final call on each suggestion.

Make sense? Let me know if you have any questions, or if this timeline doesn't work for you. Otherwise, you can expect my edits by Sunday. Looking forward!

Sending Edits

Off you go to edit. Your suggestions can be divided into two categories: global edits and line edits. Global edits are big, tectonic-level suggestions. Think: big additions, big deletions, resequencing, taking another approach with the ending, posing big questions about the plot, etc.

Line edits deal with line-level issues. These aren't just about technical correctness; you're making each line excellent, powerful, clear and concise.

Let's say you're reading Helen's essay again, and you notice a structural issue. At this point, you have a decision to make. Should you send along this global edit and wait for the writer to respond before sending along the line edits—or should you do the line editing now and send it all at once?

For us, the answer usually depends on the seismic level of the global edits. If they might significantly disrupt or reshape the manuscript, we'll send them by themselves and hold off on the line-editing. (Why polish lines that might not even be there in the next draft?) If major disruption seems unlikely, we'll send all the edits at once.

Below are two models. The first is for sending global edits by themselves; the second is for global edits and line edits together.

Model: Global Edits Only

Hi Lisa,

I just finished editing your story, and I enjoyed it all over again. <Specific compliment here> Before we get into line editing, I'd like to dig into a bigger issue.

When Michael moves away in the middle of the story, the dramatic tension seems to fizzle. Everything that's been building between him and Tristan goes up in smoke. Conveniently (maybe too conveniently?), his departure solves most of Tristan's problems. I'm wondering if the story might be more powerful if their tension came to a head instead of just dissipating. What would happen if Michael didn't move away? Or what if he came to see Tristan one last time before he left? These are just a couple of options. You might find a better way to follow through on the wonderful tension you have built between them in the first ten pages.

Would a week give you enough time to consider this revision? If you can get me another draft by next Tuesday, I'll get right on the line editing, and we'll still be on track for the May pub date. Of course, if you have any questions, or if you'd like to talk about any of this further, please let me know!

Editing is a negotiation. An editor suggests, a writer considers. An editor asks, the writer answers. If you really want a writer to listen, tell them the reason behind your suggestions. In the model above, the editor didn't tell the writer to just keep Michael in the story. Instead, the editor gave the writer a rationale, suggested some concrete possibilities, but ultimately left the solution up to the writer.

How much rationale should you offer? Here's a rule of thumb: *the bigger the suggestion, the more rationale you should offer.* If you're suggesting cutting an adverb, you might offer a few words (or none at all, trusting the writer to see the improvement). But if you're suggesting, say, a change from a linear to a non-linear timeline in the story, you're going to need to build your case, and perhaps articulate the effect the change could have on the reader.

Model: Global Edits + Line Edits

Dear Nia,

I just finished editing your piece, and I loved it even more than on my first read. The part where Rick slips his hand under the table to hold Maggie's hand while the missiles rain down on the town—oh, that wrecked me.

> Never hurts to open with a sincere compliment. Remember: You're dealing with a human with feelings here. If you demoralize the writer or piss them off, you're probably not going to get their best work in revision.

There's just one bigger structural issue I want to address. Rick slips away to the pool house with Maggie two times. Both scenes seem to serve the same purpose in the narrative: to show us how close the two are getting. But because the scenes are so similar, the second one feels redundant and slows the pace unnecessarily. What would happen if you collapsed those two scenes into a single scene? Or if the second scene did something different than the first scene? I'm sure you'll come up with an elegant solution.

> Typically, editors put global edits in the correspondence and make line edits on the manuscript.

Okay, onto line edits. My suggestions are in the document itself (see attached). Make sure to view with "final showing markup" to see the track-changes marks and the comment balloons. Accept what makes sense and reject the rest.

> Remind your writer about the "rules of the game."

If you can return a clean copy of the manuscript (without any track-changes remnants) to me by the end of February, we'll be on schedule. From there, we might go through another round of edits or we might be ready to send it to the copyeditor—I'll figure that out after I read it again, which I'm already looking forward to.

> Timeline and next steps: always, always, always.

Thanks again for such a great submission, Nia. Let me know if you have any questions about any of my suggestions, or if you'd like to talk further.

> The ending is not just a positive note, but also another "rule of the game." The writer may not know that they could talk to you about your suggestions.

Confirmation

Once you have your clean copy in hand, it's time to tie up loose ends:

- Confirmation of receipt
- Next steps
- Notes on timeline

Lisa!

I just read through your story one more time. The new scene where Tristan talks her way into a toll booth to intercept Michael on his way out of state, only to watch him zoom by in another lane—it's hilarious and heartbreaking and just what this story needed. Thank you for being willing to dig into your story so deeply.

Okay, the heavy lifting is done. From here we'll send it to the copyeditor, who will read your story with an eye toward grammar, syntax, and continuity. We'll send her suggestions your way for your approval by January 5. After you get it back to us, we'll typeset it and send it your way one final time to check for typos (which we'll be checking for, too). Finally, I'll drop you a line when your story goes live on May 1. Sound good?

It's been a pleasure to work with you, Lisa. All of us at *Little Offices* are very proud to publish "The Toll."

A Visual Recap of the Correspondence Process

Practice

To Do

Read a manuscript—either a CPR Dummy story in the appendix or another piece provided by your professor—and write a message to the writer for each step in the correspondence process. Then use the questions below to reflect.

- What kind of acceptance did you extend—and why?
- Did you separate global edits from line edits, or did you send them all together?

Explain your decision.

- What did you learn through this process? What do you still need to learn?

Case Studies

Although we're calling this section "case studies," a better (if more grisly) title might be "surgery theater." As you may have seen on TV, a surgery theater is like a lecture hall with an operating table at its heart. Surgeons in training observe an operation as it happens, usually with commentary from the surgeon performing the procedure. This observation provides a crucial link between learning from a textbook and actually using a scalpel. This link is usually missing in the education of an editor—but with our case studies, we invite you into the surgery theater of editing.

This section features six marked-up manuscripts, including the genres of poetry, short fiction, short creative nonfiction, and the chapter of a novel. The first four studies showcase different professional editors, each with a wealth of experience. The final two studies show the editing work of two undergraduate students in the process of learning the craft. As you read the studies, you'll notice a variety of editing styles. The differences in style may derive from a number of factors, including editorial temperament, training, genre, and the needs of the individual manuscript. (Once, when Bryan asked an editor if he tended to edit with a heavy hand or a light touch, the editor replied, "Whatever the manuscript requires.") Some pieces call for careful attention to the line, or global questions and suggestions, or the sound and rhythm of a writer's voice.

Each marked-up manuscript is followed by an interview with its editor. After learning from the approach and advice of these professionals, you should be more confident in your own editing approach when picking up a ~~scalpel~~ pen to practice on the sample manuscripts found in the appendix.

Julie Riddle

Creative Nonfiction/Personal Essay

Julie Riddle came to editing by way of journalism and strategic communication. Today, in addition to her day job as senior development writer at Whitworth University and editor of *Whitworth Today* magazine, Riddle is craft-essay editor for the flash-nonfiction journal

Brevity and creative-nonfiction editor for the literary magazine *Rock & Sling*. She is the rare editor who can tackle every level from global editing to copyediting, which informs her meticulous style. As you will see, Riddle engages deeply with every line of a manuscript as a way of bringing out "the music and meaning" of the essay.

Riddle is the author of the memoir *The Solace of Stones: Finding a Way through Wilderness* (University of Nebraska Press). Her essay "Shadow Animals" appeared in *The Georgia Review*; the essay received a Pushcart Prize Special Mention and was anthologized in *This Impermanent Earth* (University of Georgia Press). Her essay "If Swans Could Speak" appeared in *New England Review* (42.3). Learn more at www.julieriddle.net.

Submitted Manuscript with Editing Marks

The following manuscript was submitted by Tabitha Blankenbiller to *Brevity* in 2012. It appears below with the editing marks and comments that Riddle sent back to the writer after accepting the submission.

~~This Is Not a Book~~A Thesis Is Not a Book: Confessions of a Lutheran School Girl

Tabitha Blankenbiller

This June marks the end of my graduate work in Pacific University's low-residency MFA program. As ~~the~~a culmination of my time as a creative nonfiction student, I am compiling a thesis to convince the school that yeah, I've been writin' some stuff. ~~The distinction is often made by faculty between "thesis" and "manuscript" because as much as incoming students would like to believe otherwise, the two are not one and the same. Even if you enter the program with an elegantly-arcing personal narrative ("I was kidnapped by a bank robber who turned out to be my long-lost father"), your style and perspective in writing should evolve in a fashion so drastic that completing a viable manuscript by graduation day is unlikely at best. Like everyone else, I had to drop my delusions of walking out of commencement with a degree in one hand and a polished memoir in the other. What I will leave with is far less tangible: the craft tools and personal discipline to refine my thesis's foundation into a book outside of the structure the MFA program provides. Even the diploma won't be heading home with me; it shows up in the mail a month later.~~

So~~,~~ every morning this semester when friends, family, and my barista ask me why I look like I ~~was~~am on the wrong side of a bar fight with a raccoon~~,~~ ~~every morning this semester~~, I explain that "I'm working on my thesis." ~~My struggle to combine 40 hours of office work, at least 20 hours of school work and some passing semblance of sanity is the product of grad stress.~~ Never "I'm ~~trying to write my~~writing my book." Saying "my book," I~~'~~ve become~~m~~ convinced, is a curse. As soon as I've ever labeled a project book-worthy it falls apart. The iron masterpiece ~~I was so sure~~that stood rooted in my mind turns out to be nothing but cotton candy~~, and the rain storms in~~ in a rainstorm. ~~Keeping my work defined as~~Defining my work as a "thesis" protects the sprouts of inspiration and early drafts from falling victim to the trap of explanation. Bringing up a thesis to people sounds academic and dull, so I'm more likely to have people commiserate on their own grad work (an MBA full of theoretical accounting formulas, for instance) than ~~want to know~~ask, "So what is your book about?"

Perhaps my superstition stems from the fact that I've done this before. As an undergraduate English major, I ~~was given the option of writing~~had the option to write a gigantic literary criticism treatise, or a creative thesis to fulfill my graduation requirements. As much as spending a semester dissecting Tolstoy and combing through microfilm sounded like a total blast, I opted for the tortured artist route. *I'll write a book!* I told everyone within earshot. And if you couldn't hear me, hell yes you were getting an email.

You may have asked me what ~~it~~my book was about. Or you may have turned slightly and tried to get back to your day. Either way, I'd go on: "It's called *Confessions of a Lutheran Schoolgirl*. And it's all about how everyone tried to destroy me—*this school* tried to destroy me! But I survived."

The story covered my first two years at Concordia University, a very small liberal arts college in Portland, Oregon. The 120 pages were clobbered with every middle class coming-of-age cliché you can name: threesomes, weed, Jäagerbombs, bitchy roommates, one-night stands and handcuffs. Even better, the stock stories were conveyed with every hackneyed writing device I could dig out of my scant toolbox: Overwrought dialogue? Everywhere. Run-on~~, bad~~ Wolfe parody sentences? Well, ~~(of course)~~—I mean, my GOD! How could I write about these *craa-zy times*, man, without going a little Gaga? A chapter named with the complete transcribed lyrics of a Fiona Apple song? Check and mate.

The juvenile writing I can shrug off. I have to give my 22-year-old self a little credit; at least I was writing every single day, during hours scrounged between ~~college~~taking classes and hawking underwear at Frederick's of Hollywood. ~~As my perfectionism has grown, my production has shrunk. If I'm not going to write a gorgeous sentence, why write one at all?~~The more glaring problem with my undergrad thesis was the immediacy in the writing and in the presentation. I ~~had myself~~was convinced that I could (and should) write a memoir about events that had just happened in the last tax year. There was no concept of narrative distance and as a result, the stories never elevated ~~away from~~beyond how they would be related at happy hour. The guy was an asshole ~~and,~~ I was an innocent victim. "How could he do this to me?" I would flare, over the phone to friends and then on the page. I had no breathing room ~~in life~~ to move past the immediate, to collect these fragments of human experience and turn them around and, as Vivian Gornick demands in *The Situation and the Story*, ~~to~~ reveal "the loneliness of the monster and the cunning of the innocent." Without that ~~level of~~ bird's eye perspective looking at this clueless, lonely girl and wondering why *she* did the things she did, not what random men were doing, the narrative couldn't get off the ground. My thesis was a diary, a rehash of a crummy twenty-four months.

My book-or-nothing attitude was the first delusion I had to squash in grad school~~.~~ As Judy Blunt told me after my first MFA workshop, ~~where~~to which I'd submitted my same amateur ~~level of~~ schlock, "You need to get over this 'book' idea. That's like trying to build a house without a hammer. You need to learn how to tell a story first." The distinction is often made by MFA faculty between "thesis" and "manuscript" because, as much as incoming students would like to believe otherwise, the two are not one and the same. Even if you enter ~~the~~a grad program with an elegantly-arcing personal narrative ("I was kidnapped by a bank robber who turned out to be my long-lost father"), your style and perspective in writing should evolve in a fashion so drastic that completing a viable manuscript by graduation day is unlikely at best. Like everyone else, I had to drop my delusions of walking out of commencement with a degree in one hand and a polished memoir in the other. What I will leave with in June is far less tangible: the craft tools and personal discipline to refine my thesis's foundation into a book outside ~~of~~the structure the MFA program provides. Even the diploma won't be heading home with me; it shows up in the mail a month later.

As I slowed down, took my ~~work~~graduate writing *Bird by Bird*, I began to grow. I stopped stretching on my tiptoes for a narrative that would fill 265 pages and moved to personal essays. This allowed me to zero in on structure, on picking ~~my~~words with care, to be theatrical in doses and precise in droves. I told stories, moments, snippets well, instead of a long journey poorly. Every once ~~and~~ in a while I would get extra excited about a story and think I could blow it up~~,~~ from 15,000 words to 150,000. "A memoir of becoming a woman in the Great Recession!" or, "What it's like to be an artist in corporate America!" As soon as I said these concepts aloud, whether to a fellow writer or a civilian friend, the idea would melt.

~~"Well, you've read Jo-Ann Beard's *The Boys of My Youth*, right? It will be like that, but lighter, like *The Devil Wears Prada* MEETS *The Boys of My Youth* written by Cheryl Strayed. Because corporate work environments are really hard. . ."~~

I'm not claiming that these were ideas worth keeping. But now I'll never know, because ~~the moment~~whenever I began justifying an emerging notion, it dissolved. "Well, you've read Jo-Ann Beard's *The Boys of My Youth*, right? It will be like that, but lighter, like *The Devil Wears Prada* MEETS *The Boys of My Youth* written by Cheryl Strayed. Because corporate work environments are really hard . . ."

During my last Pacific MFA residency in Seaside, Oregon, Debra Gwartney gave a presentation on process and revision. I shuffled into the Best Western conference room thinking I knew the drill by now: ~~C~~cut! When you've cut, cut again! ~~Try reading~~Read your draft out loud. Annihilate adverbs. Instead~~, we were~~Gwartney ~~shown~~showed us a picture of a plywood skeleton, precariously held with duct tape and wood glue. "This," ~~Gwartney~~she claimed, "is a whale." The skeleton was the beginning of a sculpture by a New England artist. The artist's glimmer—*I'm going to sculpt a whale!*— was only on the path to realization. "No one can see the future whale but her," ~~explained~~Gwartney said. The sculpture's beginnings, she explained, were like our earliest drafts~~:~~: We've been inspired, we can feel and envision a final product, but all that is concrete in the world is a giant pile of wood scraps and adhesive. A long road of shaping, additions, polishes, and shavings remains before anyone else can see what we're working toward. "Which is why I would warn you against sharing your work too early," she said.

I had never considered that pushing my writing out for opinions might quell it. I get excited about a project, and I blanket my reader circle with drafts as soon as the words hit the page. *Confessions of a Lutheran Schoolgirl* had probably been read five times by all of my friends ~~when it~~before ~~was~~Concordia accepted ~~by Concordia~~it for graduation credit. What Gwartney said made the correlation between sharing and squashing click: I needed to trust myself ~~for five minutes~~to write, ponder, and rewrite before sharing my work and taking on all the doubt that keeps the universe humming.

Imagination is precious and ideas are fleeting. Even if it seems obsessive or superstitious or pathological to squirrel my work away, I'm finding the peace to draft more than worth the antisocial tendencies <u>not sharing my early work produces</u>. Premature advice can send me off the rails. I am still fleshing out, so hearing an early voice chime in with "are you sure your mother's opinion is necessary in this scene?" can set off a whole mess of destructive second-guessing. The whale, whether flash or essay or thesis or book, lives inside of me, and can't breathe out in the world unborn. Forcing myself to turn my project into a marketing elevator ~~speech~~<u>pitch</u> is the equivalent of infanticide.

So whatever is taking shape in my Word files, I love it enough to hold out. And perhaps that is the greatest thesis lesson of all: learning when to ~~shut the fuck up~~<u>keep my mouth shut</u>.

Final Version

"A Thesis Is Not a Book: Confessions of a Lutheran School Girl"
Tabitha Blankenbiller

This June marks the end of my graduate work in Pacific University's low-residency MFA program. As the culmination of my time as a creative nonfiction student, I am compiling a thesis to convince the school that yeah, I've been writin' some stuff. So, every morning this semester when friends, family, and my barista ask me why I look like I am on the wrong side of a bar fight with a raccoon, I explain that "I'm working on my thesis." Never "I'm writing my book." Saying "my book," I've become convinced, is a curse. As soon as I've ever labeled a project book-worthy it falls apart. The iron masterpiece that stood rooted in my mind turns out to be nothing but cotton candy in a rainstorm. Defining my work as a "thesis" protects the sprouts of inspiration and early drafts from falling victim to the trap of explanation. Bringing up a thesis to people sounds academic and dull, so I'm more likely to have people commiserate on their own grad work (an MBA full of theoretical accounting formulas, for instance) than ask, "So what is your book about?"

Perhaps my superstition stems from the fact that I've done this before. As an undergraduate English major, I had the option to write a gigantic literary criticism treatise or a creative thesis to fulfill my graduation requirements. As much as spending a semester dissecting Tolstoy and combing through microfilm sounded like a total blast, I opted for the tortured artist route. *I'll write a book!* I told everyone within earshot. And if you couldn't hear me, hell yes you were getting an email.

You may have asked me what my book was about. Or you may have turned slightly and tried to get back to your day. Either way, I'd go on: "It's called *Confessions of a Lutheran Schoolgirl*. And it's all about how everyone tried to destroy me—*this school* tried to destroy me! But I survived."

The story covered my first two years at Concordia University, a very small liberal arts college in Portland, Oregon. The 120 pages were clobbered with every middle class coming-of-age cliché you can name: threesomes, weed, Jägerbombs, bitchy roommates, one-night stands and handcuffs. Even better, the stock stories were conveyed with every hackneyed writing device I could dig out of my scant toolbox: Overwrought dialogue? Everywhere. Run-on Wolfe parody sentences? Well, of course —I mean, my GOD! How could I write about these *craa-zy times*, man, without going a little Gaga? A chapter named with the complete transcribed lyrics of a Fiona Apple song? Check and mate.

The juvenile writing I can shrug off. I have to give my 22-year-old self a little credit; at least I was writing every single day, during hours scrounged between taking classes and hawking underwear at Frederick's of Hollywood. The more glaring problem with my undergrad thesis was the immediacy in the writing and in the presentation. I was convinced that I could (and should) write a memoir about events that had just happened in the last tax year. There was no concept of narrative distance and as a result, the stories never elevated beyond how they would be related at happy hour. The guy was an asshole and I was an innocent victim. "How could he do this to me?" I would flare, over the phone to friends and then on the page. I had no breathing room to move past the immediate, to collect these fragments of human experience and turn them around and, as Vivian Gornick demands in *The Situation and the Story*, reveal "the loneliness of the monster and the cunning of the innocent." Without that bird's eye perspective looking at this clueless, lonely girl and wondering why *she* did the things she did, not what random men were doing, the narrative couldn't get off the ground. My thesis was a diary, a rehash of a crummy twenty-four months.

My book-or-nothing attitude was the first delusion I had to squash in grad school. As Judy Blunt told me after my first MFA workshop, to which I'd submitted my same amateur schlock, "You need to get over this 'book' idea. That's like trying to build a house without a hammer. You need to learn how to tell a story first." The distinction is often made by MFA faculty between "thesis" and "manuscript" because, as much as incoming students would like to believe otherwise, the two are not one and the same. Even if you enter a grad program with an elegantly-arcing personal narrative ("I was kidnapped by a bank robber who turned out to be my long-lost father"), your style and perspective in writing should evolve in a fashion so drastic that completing a viable manuscript by graduation day is unlikely at best. Like everyone else, I had to drop my delusions of walking out of commencement with a degree in one hand and a polished memoir in the other. What I will leave with in June is far less tangible: the craft tools and personal discipline to refine my thesis's foundation into a book outside the structure the MFA program provides. Even the diploma won't be heading home with me; it shows up in the mail a month later.

As I slowed down, took my graduate writing *Bird by Bird*, I began to grow. I stopped stretching on my tiptoes for a narrative that would fill 265 pages and moved to personal essays. This allowed me to zero in on structure, on picking words with care, to be theatrical in doses and precise in droves. I told stories, moments, snippets well, instead of a long journey poorly. Every once in a while I would get extra excited about a story and think I could blow it up from 15,000 words to 150,000. "A memoir of becoming a woman in the Great Recession!" or, "What it's like to be an artist in corporate America!" As soon as I said these concepts aloud, whether to a fellow writer or a civilian friend, the idea would melt. I'm not claiming that these were ideas worth keeping. But now I'll never know, because whenever I began justifying an emerging notion, it dissolved. "Well, you've read Jo-Ann Beard's *The Boys of My Youth,* right? It will be like that, but lighter, like *The Devil Wears Prada* MEETS *The Boys of My Youth* written by Cheryl Strayed. Because corporate work environments are really hard . . ."

During my last Pacific MFA residency in Seaside, Oregon, Debra Gwartney gave a presentation on process and revision. I shuffled into the Best Western conference room thinking I knew the drill by now: Cut! When you've cut, cut again! Read your draft out loud. Annihilate adverbs. Instead, Gwartney showed us a picture of a plywood skeleton, precariously held with duct tape and wood glue. "This," she claimed, "is a whale." The skeleton was the beginning of a sculpture by a New England artist. The artist's glimmer—*I'm going to sculpt a whale!*— was only on the path to realization. "No one can see the future whale but her," Gwartney said. The sculpture's beginnings, she explained, were like our earliest drafts: We've been inspired, we can feel and envision a final product, but all that is concrete in the world is a giant pile of wood scraps and adhesive. A long road of shaping, additions, polishes, and shavings remains before anyone else can see what we're working toward. "Which is why I would warn you against sharing your work too early," she said.

I had never considered that pushing my writing out for opinions might quell it. I get excited about a project, and I blanket my reader circle with drafts as soon as the words hit the page. *Confessions of a Lutheran Schoolgirl* had probably been read five times by all of my friends before Concordia accepted it for graduation credit. What Gwartney said made the correlation between sharing and squashing click: I needed to trust myself to write, ponder, and rewrite before sharing my work and taking on all the doubt that keeps the universe humming.

Imagination is precious and ideas are fleeting. Even if it seems obsessive or superstitious or pathological to squirrel my work away, I'm finding the peace to draft more than worth the antisocial tendencies not sharing my early work produces. Premature advice can send me off the rails. I am still fleshing out, so hearing an early voice chime in with "are you sure your mother's opinion is necessary in this scene?" can set off a whole mess of destructive second-guessing. The whale, whether flash or essay or thesis or book, lives inside of me and can't breathe out in the world unborn. Forcing myself to turn my project into a marketing elevator pitch is the equivalent of infanticide.

So whatever is taking shape in my Word files, I love it enough to hold out. And perhaps that is the greatest thesis lesson of all: learning when to keep my mouth shut.

Interview with Julie Riddle

On Beginning

I got started in editing by having my own writing edited. My first job after college was editorial assistant/reporter for *The Journal of Business*, in Spokane, Washington. The editor was a stickler for accuracy, consistency and correct grammar and punctuation. His meticulousness frustrated me, but the importance he placed on the necessity of editing to strengthen the effectiveness of writing made a lasting impression.

I didn't major in journalism in college, but my early jobs were in journalism, which taught me skills that have been valuable in editing, like not making assumptions about what seemed obvious (such as how people spell their names). I also learned to admit what I don't know. I worked for a newspaper in Nevada that covered ranching and mining, subjects I was ignorant about. During interviews, I had to ask questions—sometimes the same question multiple times—until I understood the details enough to be able to explain them to readers. Working in journalism also taught me to not make assumptions about what readers knew. My writing had to be clear, concise, informative and interesting to audiences who knew nothing about the subject as well as audiences who were familiar with the subject. Because of this, I approach editing from the perspective that I don't know anything about the subject; writers often unknowingly make assumptions in their work.

I began editing regularly when I was hired in the marketing & communications office at Whitworth University, where I started as public information officer and assistant editor of *Whitworth Today*, the university's alumni magazine. I wrote for the magazine, edited feature articles and news stories, and proofread the magazine prior to publication. I also edited content the communications office produced such as marketing publications and web text.

On Learning to Edit

> Style guide: A set of writing and formatting rules for an organization.

For the nuts-and-bolts of copyediting, I learned—and continue to learn—through daily writing and editing at Whitworth, where I now am senior development writer and editor of *Whitworth Today* magazine. I helped create a style guide for university-related subjects. Creating the style guide, updating it as the university and the world at large evolve, and applying the guide to my work have helped me think both broadly and specifically about usage, meaning and clarity. Members of the campus community also help me learn when they ask questions about grammar, punctuation or Whitworth's style, and I need to provide an answer as well as a clear explanation of the reason for that answer.

My editing experience grew to include literary editing when I began serving as craft-essay editor for the online flash-nonfiction journal *Brevity*. I screen and select essays that writers submit to *Brevity*. I identify revisions that are needed and make line edits; collaborate with the author to make these edits; and proofread the essay just prior to publication. I also became the creative-nonfiction editor for *Rock & Sling*, a literary magazine published through Whitworth University's English department. This work provides another opportunity to further hone my eye and ear for strong writing, and to make decisions about which pieces to accept, which essays merit asking the author to revise and resubmit, and which ones to decline.

The brunt of what I've learned about literary editing has come from reading widely and from writing, both of which I have done since childhood, and which I did with intense earnest as a graduate student in the Rainier Writing Workshop MFA program at Pacific Lutheran University. Reading books and writing critical analysis papers about them, and engaging—more often wrestling—with the writing process, taught me about the music and meaning of writing and how the two work in concert, and about identifying areas that falter, figuring out why, and finding solutions that strengthen the work while honoring its integrity and intent.

On Selecting Submissions for Publication

A key element of editing is deciding which submissions to accept and which ones to decline. The longer I've worked as an editor, the easier identifying submissions to decline has become. These pieces are often didactic or too simplistic, predictable or conventional; they make sweeping generalizations; they lack an engaging voice; the subject matter doesn't jibe with the journal's mission or focus; the narrative does not resonate beyond its immediate context; the essays settle for easy resolutions or trite answers.

Strong submissions are rare and often announce themselves from the first page: they take risks in form or content; they explore questions, experiences or ideas with honesty and complication; they create a sense of intimacy and anticipation with the reader; they use fresh or surprising language; they reveal a compelling mind at work on the page; they deliver on the promise offered in the opening lines. The work that falls in the middle, however, can be challenging to make decisions about. Especially when there has been a scarcity of strong submissions; the mediocre pieces can seem better than perhaps they really are, or I begin to think that maybe they could be transformed into gems with a little (more likely, a lot of) revision.

I take time to consider pieces, reading submissions several times over several days.* Clarity often comes after the second or third reading. Discussing submissions with other editors also helps sort out which essays to decline and which to accept. If my colleagues and I determine that an essay has strong potential but isn't yet complete, we identify areas that need to be addressed and I provide this feedback to the author and invite them to revise and resubmit their work.

*I learned the hard way to not rush to judgment. I once accepted an essay largely because (I realized in retrospect) I was wowed by the author's reputation and credentials. After an initial read, the piece seemed strong and I accepted it right away. Later, when I began editing the text, I realized that much of what the author had to say was vacuous and that the text was peppered with misquotes, inaccuracies and vague references. I spent a good deal of time editing the essay, and I regretted having to publish it.

Editorial Intervention

Once a submission has been accepted for publication, the process that venerable British literary editor Diana Athill calls "editorial intervention" commences. This phase of editing requires skills that can be developed and strengthened through reading a variety of genres from a critical perspective, writing and revising your own work, and gaining experience through editing others' work.

Standard "editorial intervention" includes the following:

- **Locate the strongest opening and closing sentences**. They often are not the first and last sentences of the piece. Sometimes the essay begins in the second or third paragraph, and the original opening sentences were the author clearing their throat. Sometimes an essay ends in the penultimate paragraph and the final paragraph is the author summarizing or emphasizing meaning with a pretty, but unnecessary, bow.

- **Eliminate redundancy**. Writers sometimes don't trust the reader to grasp their implicit meaning and will make their point again, explicitly. Cut that part.

- **Untangle awkward sentences**. Move, cut or add words to clarify meaning. Move a sentence or paragraph elsewhere in the piece to tighten or clarify the section it had been in and to support or enhance the section it joined. Or cut that text altogether.

- **Cut irrelevant sentences or phrases** that divert the reader's focus or that disrupt the flow of the piece. The more you read, the more you will recognize these irrelevant bits.

- **Ask the author to clarify or specify** (who is speaking? What do you mean by "it" or "things"?), **or to expand meaning** (what was the narrator's motive for taking that action?). If the author can clarify, specify or expand succinctly and artfully, so much the better.

- **Cut clutter**. A colleague once joked about academic writing, "Why say it with seven words when you can use twenty-five?" This applies to literary writing too. Give the heave-ho to flowery language, most adverbs, and intensifiers such as "very," "highly" and "extremely." Really.

- **Cut clichés and strengthen passive verbs**. They can appear at the drop of a hat.

- **Make title suggestions or ask the author to provide a more meaningful title**. Authors often slap on a bland title as an afterthought. But titles are key to catching readers' interest—they need to provide a glimpse of what's to come and spark intrigue.

On Diversity, Equity, and Inclusion

The murder of George Floyd in May 2020 ignited national and international protests, riots, debates and discussions about police brutality, institutional racism, and racial injustice. The editors of *Rock & Sling* took a hard look at our complicity in suppressing BIPOC, LGBTQ+, and other marginalized voices and experiences. Passionate discussions led to concrete actions that we committed to carrying out in sustainable and accountable ways. One of these actions was the revision of our mission statement, which we actively use to invite poetry, fiction, and creative nonfiction submissions from writers and to guide our screening of and decision-making about submissions.

A portion of our revised mission appears here, as it details the evolution from the original statement:

> *Rock & Sling* is a journal of witness, and we take that charge seriously. While in the past we have said that we are "open to experiences of all kinds," now is a time to be specific, not just open.
>
> We seek the witness, the experience, the art of Black and indigenous people and people of color. We seek the witness of genderqueer, gender fluid, and all people along the

LGBTQIA+ spectrum. We seek the witness of immigrants and refugees, of people with disabilities, of women, and of all those often marginalized by the literary and publishing communities.

. . . Witness has in its definition the concept of testimony. To testify is to tell the truth, an inherent call to all artists and writers. We seek those who are telling truth.

The more deliberate and specific language in the mission statement has led to the journal receiving and publishing increased submissions from a breadth of writers. The works often explore and interrogate an array of issues and injustices, and they provide powerful, thoughtful, and thought-provoking insights. The artists' testimonies build awareness, understanding, and a will for action.

The Editor-in-Chief of *Rock & Sling* also incorporated training in diversity, equity, and inclusion in the student-editors' course on content and developmental editing. The lead genre editors take similar training, to help ensure that our screening process is fair and equitable, and that we are more aware of how our biases factor into our decision-making process.

Suggestions for Editors

- **Read an author's cover letter *after* you've read their submission**. This helps you to focus on the quality of the writing and the strength of the narrative without being influenced by implicit biases you may hold about the writer's race, age, gender identity, sexual orientation, or publishing accomplishments (or lack of).

- **Interrogate your editorial assumptions and decisions**. As you edit, be intentional about developing an awareness of your own unconscious biases.

- **Keep an eye out for idioms, phrases with racist origins, outdated terms, and word associations that do harm**. Refer to online inclusive language style guides to inform your editing work. I recently edited a collection of essays, several of which the author had written two decades ago. I asked the author to change "stewardess" to "flight attendant" (the preferred, gender-neutral term now), and to change the once-common term "committed suicide," which has a historical, criminal connotation and reinforces a stigma, to "died by suicide," today's preferred, neutral phrase absent of shame or blame.

- **Edit from a place of humility and vulnerability**. This allows editors to be open to new ideas and approaches, to engage in candid conversations, and to become more attentive to and proficient with conscious language. As we editors grow in attentiveness and proficiency, the writing we edit will become more compelling, accurate and inclusive.

A Final Word: Guiding Principles

Following are philosophies that guide my work as an editor:

- **Approach each author's work with respect and consideration**. As a writer myself, I understand how much time, effort, and care most writers put into their work. It's tough to hand your beloved over to a stranger and trust that they have your creation's best interest at heart.

- **Editing is a collaboration and a conversation between the editor and the author**. While inaccuracies must be corrected, and unclear details and muddled meaning must be resolved, language is negotiable. I make suggestions but leave it up to the author to go with what I recommend or come up with an alternative, or they can decline an editing recommendation altogether. If I feel strongly about an edit that an author declines, I'll explain why I think it should be made and we negotiate from there.

- **Editing should support and enhance the author's voice and intent for the piece, not mine.**

- **Don't make any changes without the author's approval.**

- **Care about the small stuff.** Most of the time, the author is so close to their work that they can't see small inconsistencies or vagueness. An editor comes at the work with a clear eye and an objective perspective, so minor issues—which contribute to the overall quality of the work—stand out and should be addressed.

- **Keep your ego in check**. The editor's job is behind the scenes; the author gets credit for the work. In *Stet: An Editor's Life*, Diana Athill writes, "An editor must never expect thanks (sometimes they come, but they must always be seen as a bonus). We must always remember that we are only midwives—if we want praise for progeny, we must give birth to our own."

In my experience, most authors appreciate having an attentive editor spend time on their writing and they are agreeable to sensible changes. They often express surprise at how much stronger the piece becomes.

Editing is gratifying work: The process allows me to engage with interesting and talented writers and to learn from them; to develop and sharpen my skills—both editing and writing; to publish works that have a meaningful impact on readers; and to participate in literary citizenship. Plus, I get to have fun playing with words.

To Consider

1 Regarding Riddle's editing, what do you notice? How would you describe her editing style?

2 What surprised you?

3 What can you learn from this case study?

4 As an editor, is there anything you might have done differently with this piece— either in terms of general approach or any individual choices? (Your answer to this question might reveal a good deal about your own editing style and sensibility.)

5 What questions do you have after reading this case study?

Valerie Vogrin

Creative Nonfiction/Personal Essay

When the writer George Saunders revises his own work, he reads over the text and "imagine[s] a little meter in [his] head, with 'P' on one side ('Positive') and 'N' on the other ('Negative')." He pays attention to his reactions. When the needle on his meter swings over to "N," he revises accordingly.

> For more about his approach, see Saunders' book, *A Swim in the Pond in the Rain*.

Valerie Vogrin, managing editor and prose editor of *Sou'wester*, employs a similar technique in her editing practice. "The most creative part of editing occurs when I focus on small moments of letdown," says Vogrin, referring to "places where [she] feel[s] the energy or intensity or precision of the story flag." As an editor, Vogrin is like a skilled practitioner of acupressure, putting her finger on key places for the writer to revisit and revise.

In addition to her editing work, Vogrin is also a writer. Her collection *Things We'll Need for the Coming Difficulties* was awarded the Spokane Prize for Short Fiction (Willow Springs Press, 2020). She is the author of the novel *Shebang*, and her short stories have appeared in journals such as *Ploughshares*, *AGNI*, *Hobart*, and *The Los Angeles Review*. She's a professor of creative writing at Southern Illinois University Edwardsville.

Submitted Manuscript with Editing Marks

The following manuscript was submitted by Colin Rafferty to *Sou'wester*. It appears below with the editing marks and comments that Vogrin sent back to the writer after accepting the submission.

This Day in History

That's kind of a pre-September 10th mentality, the hope
that somehow resolutions and failed inspections would make
this world a more peaceful place.

--George W. Bush, responding to John Kerry's
criticism at the first 2004 presidential debate

September 10, 1776: Nathan Hale volunteers to spy for the Continental Army.

> Is "statute" instead of "statue" your typo or the entrant's?

> We will start with the palm (hollow of the hand), which holds the City of New York in detail (the twin towers, a statute of Mayor Giuliani, firefighters, etc) and is encased with the Pentagon as a base with a seagull at the top corner. The White House is engraved in the front of the base with the US flag. All of the armed forces are represented. (entry 683975)

> The garden of peace could be in one section or in two sections on either side of the walkway of the river of peace. The unidentified remains may be put in this contemplation area. The walk can include a walkway with peace in many languages engraved in the stones—for example, peace—USA, shalom—Israel, etc. Benches and seating places would be apparent throughout the garden, as well as weeping willows, weeping cherry trees and flowering trees such as crabapple and red bud, etc. to depict hope. The area would be surrounded by many varieties of the peace rose to go with the theme of the garden of peace as well as other appropriate plants and bushes. (entry 683984)

I've been to New York City once in thirty-five years, so it's a little odd for me to presume that I could write anything about what to do with Ground Zero, or to critique what has been done with the site. I never saw the World Trade Center, except on television or in photographs, and it was on television and in photographs that I watched it destroyed.

I remember that when I saw the South Tower drop, I thought, "Wwell, they could probably rebuild one of them," and when the North Tower fell, I was watching C-SPAN (though by that point, every channel was the same) and they didn't say anything about it as it happened. A caller was going on about something—I don't remember what—and they didn't stop him.

September 10, 1913: The Lincoln Highway, America's first coast-to-coast highway, opens.

I have a joke: I lived in Manhattan for four years, but—wait for it—it was Manhattan, Kansas, which bills itself as "The Little Apple." Seriously. I guess if Anderson Hall on the campus of Kansas State University was attacked and destroyed, I might have an idea for what to do for a memorial, or at least feel more attached to what was built there.

When I've been close enough to New York City to see highway signs for it, I've been surprised, like I've seen a sign that says "Mars: 250 miles." The city feels that remote to me. Television and movies don't really endear me to the town; it frustrates me with its omnipresence, how everything's set there, how everything seems to revolve around it, and how it sometimes mocks where I'm from, something about a flyover state or a Toto joke.

September 10, 1945: Vidkun Quisling is sentenced to die for collaborating with the Nazis in Norway.

I'd guess, though, that a lot of the people who submitted designs for the WTC memorial have never been to NYC, either. I mean, 5,201 submissions is a lot. And not all of them are by certified architects; there are <u>entries with bad grammar,</u> freehand drawings, ~~and bad grammar~~and handwritten descriptions.

> The Garden of the Moment takes the idealized form of the footprint of the tower that once stood in its place. The charred, bent and deformed outer shell wraps the garden. Most of the footprint has an open lawn, except in the location of its former core which contains fractured columns, and stairs which took so many to safety, now standing as elements. Within the area that was the core are four large pylons each evoking some aspect of the moment. The first encases a flame eternal and powerful. The second, billowing smoke and everlasting darkness. The Third contains objects of daily life thrown to the wind, bills, pictures, and memos swirling around in a vortex. The final Pylon contains video and still images a simple representation of how this event was tied to the world and the world to this spot. (entry 683610)

I find it difficult~~, now,~~ to remember what it felt like that day. I remember it was nice outside. I remember my clock radio woke me up with the news of the second tower being hit. I remember being grateful to find a coffeeshop that afternoon that didn't have its television on. I remember seeing a man walking down the street, carrying an American flag, and flashing the peace sign to honking cars. That seems odd, now.

> The chronology of your account could be made a bit more clear, I think. You woke up to the news then turned on the TV and saw the towers falling on C-SPAN.

September 10, 1990: Iran and Iraq resume diplomatic ties.

And this is the trouble with trying to build a memorial for it, with trying to fix that moment in time: so much history has <u>built on</u> top of it, even in the short time since. When I visited the Flight 93 crash site in Shanksville, we weren't in Iraq yet. Now, September 11th and the Iraq war seem impossibly linked, one as the excuse for the other.

> Best way to say this? "Accrued" maybe?

Every day is history.

Every day is ordinary.

September 10, 1919: General John J. Pershing and 25,000 soldiers are welcomed with a parade in New York City.

> The central theme for this proposed memorial design is the individual recognition of each and every victim at the site. A sculptor will be commissioned to create a likeness of each person's face out of stone or bronze. Each face will be shown in relief within a uniform sized block. (Approximately, one foot square per block.) The name, place of birth and birthday for each victim will be inscribed on the block. (entry 683256)

For instance, my birthday. March 25th probably passes unnoticed for you each year, but for me, it's a significant date. If you're Catholic, you know it's the Annunciation. If you're a history buff, you know it's the anniversary of the Triangle Shirtwaist Factory fire. But for most people, it's 24 hours of their lives, the regular twists and turns of daily existence.

> The labyrinth will be located in the south one-half of the north footprint. The path describing the labyrinth's patterns will be 27-inches wide to accommodate the handicapped, with 4-inches of grass between paths. The labyrinth's center will consist of a 6-foot square containing an eternal flame. The paths will be lined with ground, crushed and polished rose quartz crystal. Rose quartz is a healing stone, associated with the heart. It will bring healing energy to it. The labyrinth will cover a 66-square area, place within a 74-diameter circle. Add a 10-foot wide concrete walkway to the perimeter of the circle, with benches and lighting interspersed at intervals. The north foot print will have lighting around its perimeter as well, and landscaping throughout the area. (entry 350019)

> [Not exactly. Many people on the East Coast were well into their day. For West Coasters the news came in late morning; someone came running into a meeting and we pulled out a TV to find out what was going on.]

But this event, the one we're trying to memorialize, it happened to all of us; everyone tuned in as they woke up that morning, like a curtain drawn across the country.

September 10, 1955: "Gunsmoke" premieres on CBS.

And we saw it happen. Now, we don't see it much; it's like it's kept from us. It was odd, each year, to see the footage again, on the anniversaries.

> [This could be sharper, more precise. It was difficult to not see it initially (by choice, I have never watched the towers fall). Now, to me, it seems like it's stored away for safekeeping until the anniversaries. Your experience is unique, of course, but I'd just like you to make your sense of things more distinct.]

> The footprint of the South Tower is marked by a granite enclosure that rises above the height of the upper street level. It is a brooding, anonymous object, whose gravity is evident by the canted walls that loom over visitors. The entry is marked by a modest slot that is sliced through the black granite face. Set in front of the waterfall, this enclosure acts to contain the power of the rushing water: a sound barrier between the tower footprint and the rest of the memorial site. Within, it becomes an amphitheater—a series of concentric steps of black granite radiating upwards from a 50' by 50' central plaza. In contrast to one's initial perception, as one climbs the steps to the top, each row of stairs reveals itself to be inset with grass, invisible to visitors from below. Each grass face provides a comfortable seating area for individuals to contemplate the sight and sound of the waterfall. (entry 122599)

In 2006, on CNN's website, visitors could watch the live footage from that morning five years earlier, as it happened. I found it interesting how long it takes the anchors to realize what's happening; even after the second plane hits, they still theorize that maybe it's an air traffic navigation malfunction. There's not a little denial and disbelief at work in their voices.

> [Blah word. Interesting how? How do you feel about their denial and disbelief? Is this poignant – this clinging to ignorance for a few more seconds or minutes?]

For me, watching it five years later, there was not a little regret. It was, after all, what had led us to where we are now, in the midst of a withdrawal that may or may not ever end in a country not connected to the original attack.

> [I'd suggest deleting this or, as I wrote above, tightening the prose to make more clear what you felt at the five year marker. I can't be sure of the tone of "not a little regret."]

September 10, 1608: John Smith becomes president of the Jamestown colony in Virginia.

~~We~~Each of us started out somewhere~~,~~ and ~~we~~ended up somewhere else, and ~~now,~~ looking back, it's difficult to remember how we felt when we started. I haven't lived in Kansas for thirteen years. I don't remember what it's like to be there.

> The chime tower and the display of individual photographs are meant to memorialize people as individuals. The chime tower will use music to symbolize the victims' spirits that will always live on in the lives of their loved ones. The chime tower will play uniquely created music as well as provide a special type of visual physical representation of the huge number of lives lost. the tower displays 3022 chimes (one for each victim) each with a unique design (color and shape) and with each producing a unique sound. (entry 122134)

So many of the proposals discuss ~~how they want~~the desire for the memorial to heal the country, to relieve the suffering they ascribe to all of us, but especially to the victims' families.

> Does the above capture your meaning? Or are you speaking only of people in the US or some other specific "we"?

September 10, 1924: A jury declares Leopold and Loeb guilty of murder.

There's a <u>frequently expressed</u> wish~~, often,~~ to bring the nation back together, to halt time at the point when we were still together, before everything fell apart, before we lost the way. That's a difficult project for a memorial, especially when many of the most successful memorials were built over someone's objection<u>considerable controversy and complaint</u>. And there are already so many restrictions on the

> Might you interrogate this further. I think, for example, when was that exactly – when were we together, when were things whole, when did we have our way?

> Is this word needed? What do you mean by "successful"?

> The remainder of the site is entirely paved with limestone and no landscaping is added to define this subterranean urban space. The memorial is one that emphasizes the sheer volume of senseless murders achieved during these acts of terrorism. The scale and detailing fill but do not overwhelm the site and keep the proportions on a manageable human dimension. Hopefully, this serene and uncomplicated design will heal a grieving nation. (entry 446243)

> This is a good point, but perhaps belongs in a different section. Here you're focusing on the crazy ambition of the proposals.

memorial's design—it must preserve the footprints of the towers, it must provide a space for unidentified remains, it must feature a private space for the victims' families—that to add unifying the country to the to-do list seems a little optimistic.

> Understatement doesn't work here, to my ear.

The site itself rebels against being fixed in time. Workers in 2006, opening some manholes for the first time since the attack, found human remains. Like a Civil War battlefield, the World Trade Center still holds its dead close to itself.

I keep thinking about paper memorials: the posters of the missing plastering the walls of New York City, the special editions of newspapers with their 120-point headlines. Most of all, I keep thinking about the paper that fell from the sky that day, ephemera of corporate life burned at the edges. I keep thinking about how in a stockholder report, a blank page is never blank, never empty; instead, at the bottom, small type ~~reads~~<u>announces</u> this page intentionally left blank.

The void acknowledged, the absence felt. In 2001, I had never been to New York City, but I ~~still~~nevertheless felt sorrow and fear that day. I felt sorrow and fear that day, but I hide that now.

September 10, 1734: British clergyman George Whitefield writes, "Pain, if patiently endured, and sanctified to us, is a great purifier of our corrupted nature."

The design concept start from the statue of liberty, drawing an imaginary line from liberty to the site with 2 lines of **lights**. Reaching to the site the lights turn into **water—*a symbol of light, innocent and life***—then a **waterfall** will guide the water down to the ground Zero, which the **wall** holding the water fall will serve as a separate accesible space to serve as a final resting-place for the unidentified remains from the World Trade Center site. In the lower level there is a **wide space** surrounding water which serves as an space for contemplation. in the continuing of the water is the **frame**, *the frame contains the name of the victims on it's body* and is holding the American **flag painting** that stand high, it is a symbol of 2 towers who are united on top. The tall frame holds the painting—both site of the plate contain the same painting—that represent an original and powerful statement of enduring and unifying symbolism. (entry 350023)

We decided that the remains should not be relegated to some corner, but made the gravitational center of the memorial. That is what matters; it is the lives that made this place sacred. Thus we envisioned a single, central grave extending along one side of the south-tower footprint. Beneath the line would be buried the unidentified remains. (entry 089005)

A lot of the proposals don't make much sense.

September 10, 1981: Picasso's "Guernica" returns to Spain.

Which might be a legitimate response.

My favorite proposal is one that I heard just a few days afterwards. Tear it all down, the artist said, level it off, and plant native grasses. Establish a bison herd on the site, restoring some of what once was to the commotion of lower Manhattan. I like this because it takes the impulse to push the clock back to its logical extreme: remove human involvement from the site. Humans did this to other humans; the best way to memorialize the site, to honor the victims, is to return to the time before humans ~~did things to~~harmed other humans. It is to write, in a way, this site intentionally left blank.

September 10, 1939: Canada declares war on Germany.

As far as I know, that proposal was never officially submitted. And probably for good reason; even when there were only four people on Earth, one of them was a murderer and one of them was a victim.

When I visit, some day, the World Trade Center memorial in New York City, I will peer into the curtain of water and at the ribbon of names, and in their movement, I will see history fixed in place. I will tell my family—a family that does not exist as I write this, on this day in history—

Bordering each pool is a pair of ramps that lead down to the memorial spaces. Descending into the memorial, visitors are removed from the sights and sounds of the city and immersed in a cool darkness. As they proceed, the sound of water falling grows louder, and more daylight filters in from below. At the bottom of the descent, they find themselves behind a thin curtain of water, staring out at an enormous pool. Surrounding this pool is a continuous ribbon of names. The enormity of this space and the multitude of names that form this endless ribbon underscore the vast scope of the destruction. Standing there at the water's edge, looking at a pool of water that is flowing away into an abyss, a visitor to the site can sense that what is beyond this curtain of water and ribbon of names is inaccessible. (entry 790532 [winning entry])

A more clear description here?

about how I woke up to my clock radio's news, how I watched the towers fall live on television. I will tell them how I felt that day, and in the months and years afterwards, how the event changed with other events, each one's gravitational pull affecting the other. We will watch the water fall, disappearing into the abyss, and maybe I will be reminded of the towers falling. Maybe I will be reminded of 5,200 unbuilt memorials.

faux abyss?

Maybe I will remember how, one day in college, driving outside the Little Apple, I came upon a field of bison. Several were standing next to the fence's gate, and when I parked my car and stood next to one, I could look into its eye, a single glassy black orb in which I could see nothing reflected.

This is a terrific ending. I think it would be even stronger if this moment was a bit more fully realized.

Final Version
Sou'wester

COLIN RAFFERTY

This Day in History

> *That's kind of a pre-September 10th mentality, the hope that somehow resolutions and failed inspections would make this world a more peaceful place.*
> *--George W. Bush, responding to John Kerry's criticism at the first 2004 presidential debate*

SEPTEMBER 10, 1776: NATHAN HALE VOLUNTEERS TO SPY FOR THE CONTINENTAL ARMY.

I've been to New York City once in thirty-five years, so it's a little odd for me to presume that I could write anything about what to do with Ground Zero, or to critique what has been done with the site. I never saw the World Trade Center, except on television or in photographs, and it was on television and in photographs that I watched it destroyed.

> ```
> We will start with the palm (hollow
> of the hand), which holds the City
> of New York in detail (the twin
> towers, a statute [sic] of Mayor
> Giuliani, firefighters, etc) and is
> encased with the Pentagon as a base
> with a seagull at the top corner.
> The White House is engraved in the
> front of the base with the US
> flag. All of the armed forces are
> represented.
> ```
> (entry 683975)

I remember that when I saw the South Tower drop, I thought, "Well, they could probably rebuild one of them," and when the North Tower fell, I was watching C-SPAN (though by that point, every channel was the same) and they didn't say anything about it as it happened. A caller was going on about something—I don't remember what—and they didn't stop him.

SEPTEMBER 10, 1913: THE LINCOLN HIGHWAY, AMERICA'S FIRST COAST-TO-COAST HIGHWAY, OPENS.

I have a joke: I lived in Manhattan for four years, but—wait for it—it was Manhattan, Kansas, which bills itself as "The Little Apple." Seriously. I guess if Anderson Hall on the campus of Kansas State University was attacked and destroyed, I might have an idea for what to do for a memorial, or at least feel more attached to what was built there.

When I've been close enough to New York City to see highway signs for it, I've been surprised, like I've seen a sign that says "Mars: 250 miles." The city feels that remote to me. Television and movies don't really endear me to the town; it frustrates me with its omnipresence, how everything's set there, how everything seems to revolve around it, and how it sometimes mocks where I'm from, something about a flyover state or a Toto joke.

4

September 10, 1945: Vidkun Quisling is sentenced to die for collaborating with the Nazis in Norway.

> The garden of peace could be in one section or in two sections on either side of the walkway of the river of peace. The unidentified remains may be put in this contemplation area. The walk can include a walkway with peace in many languages engraved in the stones--for example, peace--USA, shalom--Israel, etc. Benches and seating places would be apparent throughout the garden, as well as weeping willows, weeping cherry trees and flowering trees such as crabapple and red bud, etc. to depict hope. The area would be surrounded by many varieties of the peace rose to go with the theme of the garden of peace as well as other appropriate plants and bushes.
>
> (entry 683984)

I'd guess, though, that a lot of the people who submitted designs for the WTC memorial have never been to NYC, either. I mean, 5,201 submissions is a lot. And not all of them are by certified architects; there are entries with bad grammar, freehand drawings, and handwritten descriptions.

I find it difficult to remember what it felt like that day. I remember it was nice outside. I remember my clock radio woke me up with the news of the second tower being hit. I remember turning on the television, flipping through the channels as they all interrupted their coverage, ending up on C-SPAN for no reason at all. I remember being grateful to find a coffeeshop that afternoon that didn't have its television on. I remember seeing a man walking down the street, carrying an American flag, and flashing the peace sign to honking cars. That seems odd, now.

September 10, 1990: Iran and Iraq resume diplomatic ties.

> The Garden of the Moment takes the idealized form of the footprint of the tower that once stood in its place. The charred, bent and deformed outer shell wraps the garden. Most of the footprint has an open lawn, except in the location of its former core which contains fractured columns, and stairs which took so many to safety, now standing as elements. Within the area that was the core are four large pylons each evoking some aspect of the moment. The first encases a flame eternal and powerful. The second, billowing smoke and everlasting darkness. The Third contains objects of daily life thrown to the wind, bills, pictures, and memos swirling around in a vortex. The final Pylon contains video and still images a simple representation of how this event was tied to the world and the world to this spot.
>
> (entry 683610)

Sou'wester

And this is the trouble with trying to build a memorial for it, with trying to fix that moment in time: so much history has accrued, even in the short time since. When I visited the Flight 93 crash site in Shanksville, we weren't in Iraq yet. Now, September 11th and the Iraq war seem impossibly linked, one as the excuse for the other.

Every day is history.

Every day is ordinary.

SEPTEMBER 10, 1919: GENERAL JOHN J. PERSHING AND 25,000 SOLDIERS ARE WELCOMED WITH A PARADE IN NEW YORK CITY.

```
The central theme for this proposed
memorial design is the individual
recognition of each and every victim
at the site. A sculptor will be
commissioned to create a likeness of
each person's face out of stone or
bronze. Each face will be shown in
relief within a uniform sized block.
(Approximately, one foot square per
block.)  The name, place of birth
and birthday for each victim will be
inscribed on the block.
                        (entry 683256)
```

For instance, my birthday. March 25th probably passes unnoticed for you each year, but for me it's a significant date. If you're Catholic, you know it's the Annunciation. If you're a history buff, you know it's the anniversary of the Triangle Shirtwaist Factory fire. But for most people, it's twenty-four hours of their lives, the regular twists and turns of daily existence.

But this event, the one we're trying to memorialize, it happened to all of us; whether it interrupted our morning or greeted us when we woke, we watched it, gravitating towards television screens, then, in disbelief, gravitating towards each other, trying to make something out of what we had witnessed.

```
The labyrinth will be located in the south one-half of the north
footprint. The path describing the labyrinth's patterns will be 27-
inches wide to accommodate the handicapped, with 4-inches of grass
between paths. The labyrinth's center will consist of a 6-foot
square containing an eternal flame. The paths will be lined with
ground, crushed and polished rose quartz crystal. Rose quartz is
a healing stone, associated with the heart. It will bring healing
energy to it. The labyrinth will cover a 66-square area, place
within a 74-diameter circle. Add a 10-foot wide concrete walkway to
the perimeter of the circle, with benches and lighting interspersed
at intervals. The north foot print will have lighting around its
perimeter as well, and landscaping throughout the area.
                                                    (entry 350019)
```

SEPTEMBER 10, 1955:
GUNSMOKE PREMIERES
ON CBS.

And we saw it happen.
Now, I don't see it much;
it's like it's gone from
the specific act to a
remembered date. I find
it odd, each year, to see
the footage again, on
the anniversaries, the
moments of impact,
the collapse, the sudden
remembering of that
single day.

In 2006, on CNN's
website, visitors could
watch the live footage
from that morning
five years earlier, as it

> The footprint of the South Tower is marked
> by a granite enclosure that rises above the
> height of the upper street level. It is a
> brooding, anonymous object, whose gravity
> is evident by the canted walls that loom
> over visitors. The entry is marked by a
> modest slot that is sliced through the black
> granite face. Set in front of the waterfall,
> this enclosure acts to contain the power
> of the rushing water: a sound barrier
> between the tower footprint and the rest
> of the memorial site. Within, it becomes an
> amphitheater--a series of concentric steps
> of black granite radiating upwards from a
> 50' by 50' central plaza. In contrast to
> one's initial perception, as one climbs the
> steps to the top, each row of stairs reveals
> itself to be inset with grass, invisible to
> visitors from below. Each grass face provides
> a comfortable seating area for individuals
> to contemplate the sight and sound of the
> waterfall.
>
> (entry 122599)

happened: the anchors take a long time to realize what's happening; even after the second
plane hits, they still theorize that maybe it's an air traffic navigation malfunction. There's
not a little denial and disbelief at work in their voices. For me, watching it five years
later, I felt only regret and sorrow, both for the day, and for what I knew would follow.

SEPTEMBER 10, 1608: JOHN SMITH BECOMES PRESIDENT OF THE JAMESTOWN
COLONY IN VIRGINIA.

Each of us started out somewhere and ended up somewhere else, and looking back,
it's difficult to remember how we felt when we started. I haven't lived in Kansas for over

> The chime tower and the display of individual photographs are meant
> to memorialize people as individuals. The chime tower will use
> music to symbolize the victims' spirits that will always live on in
> the lives of their loved ones. The chime tower will play uniquely
> created music as well as provide a special type of visual physical
> representation of the huge number of lives lost. the tower displays
> 3022 chimes (one for each victim) each with a unique design (color
> and shape) and with each producing a unique sound.
>
> (entry 122134)

Sou'wester

> ```
> The remainder of the site is entirely
> paved with limestone and no landscaping
> is added to define this subterranean
> urban space. The memorial is one that
> emphasizes the sheer volume of senseless
> murders achieved during these acts of
> terrorism. The scale and detailing
> fill but do not overwhelm the site and
> keep the proportions on a manageable
> human dimension. Hopefully, this serene
> and uncomplicated design will heal a
> grieving nation.
>
>                          (entry 446243)
> ```

a decade. I don't remember what it's like to be there.

So many of the proposals discuss the desire for the memorial to heal the country, to relieve the suffering they ascribe to all of us, but especially to the victims' families.

SEPTEMBER 10, 1924: A JURY DECLARES LEOPOLD AND LOEB GUILTY OF MURDER.

There's a frequently expressed wish to bring the nation back together, to halt time at the point when we were still together, before everything fell apart, before we lost the way. And either they're idealizing the time before September 11th, as fractous and divided as any other, or they're idealizing the days immediately after, the not-quite-month before we invaded Afghanistan. They're remembering the flags waving from what seemed like every house; they're remembering the lines of Americans waiting to donate blood. That's a difficult project for a memorial—trying trying bring the country back to a time that barely existed, that maybe never existed—after all, the Red Cross, overwhelmed with donations, threw out thousands of gallons of blood that they couldn't store. And the competition placed so many restrictions on the memorial's design—it must preserve the footprints of the towers, it must provide a space for unidentified remains, it must feature a private space for the victims' families—that to add "unify the country" to the to-do list seems a little optimistic.

The site itself rebels against being fixed in time. Workers in 2006, opening some manholes for the first time since the attack, found human remains. Like a Civil War battlefield, the World Trade Center still holds its dead close to itself.

I keep thinking about paper memorials: the posters of the missing plastering the walls of New York City, the special editions of newspapers with their 120-point headlines. Most of all, I keep thinking about the paper that fell from the sky that day, ephemera of corporate life burned at the edges. I keep thinking about how in a stockholder report, a blank page is never blank, never empty; instead, at the bottom, small type announces this page intentionally left blank.

Fall 2013

The void acknowledged, the absence felt. In 2001, I had never been to New York City, but I nevertheless felt sorrow and fear that day. I felt sorrow and fear that day, but I hide that now.

SEPTEMBER 10, 1734: BRITISH CLERGYMAN GEORGE WHITEFIELD WRITES, "PAIN, IF PATIENTLY ENDURED, AND SANCTIFIED TO US, IS A GREAT PURIFIER OF OUR CORRUPTED NATURE."

A lot of the proposals don't make much sense.

SEPTEMBER 10, 1981: PICASSO'S "GUERNICA" RETURNS TO SPAIN.

Which might be a legitimate response.

My favorite proposal is one that I heard just a few days afterwards. Tear it all down, the artist said, level it off, and plant native grasses. Establish a bison herd on the site, restoring some of what once was to the commotion of lower Manhattan. I like this because it takes the impulse to push the clock back to its logical extreme: remove human involvement from the site. Humans did this to other humans; the best way to memorialize the site, to honor the victims, is to return to the time before humans harmed other humans. It is to write, in a way, this site intentionally left blank.

SEPTEMBER 10, 1939: CANADA DECLARES WAR ON GERMANY.

```
The design concept start from the
statue  of  liberty,  drawing  an
imaginary line from liberty to the
site with 2 lines of lights. Reaching
to  the  site  the  lights  turn  into
water--a symbol of light, innocent
and  life--then  a  waterfall  will
guide the water down to the ground
Zero,  which  the  wall  holding  the
water fall will serve as a separate
accesible  space  to  serve  as  a  final
resting-place  for  the  unidentified
remains from the World Trade Center
site.  In  the  lower  level  there  is  a
wide space  surrounding  water  which
serves as an space for contemplation.
in  the  continuing  of  the  water  is
the  frame,  the  frame  contains  the
name of the victims on it's body and
is holding the American flag painting
that stand high, it is a symbol of
2 towers who are united on top. The
tall frame holds the painting--both
site  of  the  plate  contain  the  same
painting--that represent an original
and  powerful  statement  of  enduring
and unifying symbolism.
                    (entry 350023)
```

As far as I know, that proposal was never officially submitted. And probably for good reason; even when there were only four people on Earth, one of them was a murderer and one of them was a victim.

When I visit, some day, the World Trade Center memorial in New York City, dedicated on the tenth anniversary of the attacks, I will peer into the curtain of water and at the ribbon of names, and running my hand over the engraved letters, spelling out

Sou'wester

We decided that the remains should not be
relegated to some corner, but made the
gravitational center of the memorial.
That is what matters; it is the lives
that made this place sacred. Thus we
envisioned a single, central grave
extending along one side of the south-
tower footprint. Beneath the line would
be buried the unidentified remains.

(entry 089005)

one of thousands of names,
I will see history fixed in
place. I will tell my family—a
family that does not exist as
I write this, on this day in
history—about how I woke up
to my clock radio's news, how I
watched the towers fall live on
television. I will tell them how I
felt that day, and in the months
and years afterwards, how the
event changed with other events, each one's gravitational pull affecting the other. We will
watch the water fall, disappearing into the preserved abyss of each tower's footprint, and
maybe I will be reminded of the towers falling. Maybe I will be reminded of 5,200 unbuilt memorials.

Maybe I will remember how, one day in college, driving outside the Little Apple, I came upon a field of bison. Several stood next to the fence's gate, quietly grazing. I parked my car nearby and walked towards them, trying not to scare the animals. As I approached, they did not move away, and I found myself face-to-face with a single bison, with only the bars of the gate between us. I looked into the bison's

Bordering each pool is a pair of ramps that lead down to the memorial
spaces. Descending into the memorial, visitors are removed from
the sights and sounds of the city and immersed in a cool darkness.
As they proceed, the sound of water falling grows louder, and
more daylight filters in from below. At the bottom of the descent,
they find themselves behind a thin curtain of water, staring out
at an enormous pool. Surrounding this pool is a continuous ribbon
of names. The enormity of this space and the multitude of names
that form this endless ribbon underscore the vast scope of the
destruction. Standing there at the water's edge, looking at a pool
of water that is flowing away into an abyss, a visitor to the site
can sense that what is beyond this curtain of water and ribbon of
names is inaccessible.

(entry 790532 [winning entry])

10

Fall 2013

eye. I wanted to see history, the billions of bison that once roamed the entire continent. I wanted to see the power that I knew dwelled in the bison's enormous frame. I wanted to see survival, the continuation of a species that man almost destroyed.

I wanted to see all these things, but on that day in Kansas, quiet and sunny, when I looked into its eye, I saw only a single glassy black orb in which I could see nothing reflected.

Interview with Valerie Vogrin

On Beginning

My first experience in editing was as co-founding editor of a student literary journal at my undergraduate alma mater, Washington State University, *Wind Row* (now defunct). I confess I don't remember all that much about the experience. In retrospect what stands out is how different the process was back then. All the submissions were hard copies and most of the production process was in the hands of paid staff.

My next editing experience was as a reader for *Black Warrior Review* at University of Alabama. This was significantly different, obviously—working on the staff of a journal with a national readership. It was the first time I realized that literary journals were really a thing. Being part of an editing team meant that I had to learn how to argue for or against a story, which was much different than making decisions by decree.

One Approach to Editing

First, I should say that I'm hesitant to accept pieces that need a lot of editing. Working on such pieces, no matter how much potential I see, feels like borrowing trouble. I want to avoid a situation in which I ask a writer to make changes and the writer makes them in good faith, but in doing so creates another "problem," resulting in frustration on both sides (particularly the writer's). Thus, I try to limit myself to accepting stories and essays that I would be willing to print more or less as is, but that I think would be improved by minor changes. Very occasionally I'm willing to engage a writer in a discussion about more significant changes if I have a strong sense the writer will really get what I'm saying. There's some instinct involved here, but the sophistication of the writing is a good indicator. If I'm familiar with the writer's other work, that could sway me, too.

As an editor, I try to practice restraint. My job isn't to shape the writer's original into the piece I would have written. I try to respect writers' choices, honoring their idiosyncrasies regarding word choice and sentence structure, for instance. I point to what seem to me to be infelicities of language and areas of confusion. (I try not to worry about feeling stupid when I question something I think might be obvious to another reader!)

The most creative part of editing occurs when I focus on small moments of letdown—places where I feel the energy or intensity or precision of the story flag. Sometimes I have a suggestion and sometimes I just hope the writer can figure it out. Throughout the process, I emphasize that I am only making suggestions. At the same time, if I don't think something is working (such as a title that puts my teeth on edge) I try to come right out with it, as respectfully as possible. I've found that writers (including myself) appreciate the time and attention. So far so good—as far as I know there have been only good feelings between me and the writers I work with.

Why Edit

As I mentioned previously, I've been involved with literary editing on and off since my twenties. I am fascinated and impressed by the enormous variety of literary journals that exist in the world. It's been exciting to see the rise of the online journal. The kind of exposure that those journals and the online presence of print journals offers writers is a real boon. As a reader, I love that there are so many ways to find great work! (Back in the olden days I used to send off checks for $5 and $6 to purchase sample copies of the journals I located in the back page listings of the *Best American* series.)

So it's an honor, really, to play a role in the larger literary landscape. I'm still amazed that so many talented writers have sent *Sou'wester* their best work—work that when published garnered them about $30 worth of contributor's copies!

To be involved with an international community that is powered largely by labors of love aligns with my personal and political beliefs. Just as I have given my time to *Sou'wester* to help writers connect to readers, many hundreds of other people donate their time and money to publish chapbooks, online and print journals, and literary books of every sort. My first novel was edited by a volunteer at a university press. Almost all of my own stories that have appeared in journals and anthologies did so thanks to other people's generosity.

On Diversity, Equity, and Inclusion

In the aftermath of the killing of George Floyd and nationwide discussions about institutional racism, we joined a host of literary organizations and journals in some serious soul-searching. Our realization was stark and painful. While editors past and present had welcomed work by BIPOC writers as well as LGBTQ writers, we clearly had not taken sufficient steps to remedy the lack of diversity in *Sou'wester*, particularly its overwhelming whiteness.

In collaboration with graduate student assistant editors, we crafted a new mission statement: *The editors of* Sou'wester *have examined past issues and acknowledge the lack of diverse writers and stories. We understand how this feeds into gatekeeping and silencing. We are committed to investing in and encouraging the words/stories/voices of all writers, prioritizing those belonging to marginalized communities.* Through our social media and several paid advertisements, we disseminated our revised call for submissions.

In the short term, we achieved some success. The issue we published in Spring 2021 was *Sou'wester*'s most diverse ever. For example, we published five BIPOC writers in addition to four emerging black poets featured in a special section curated by our colleague Dr. Howard Rambsy.

This experience caused us to rethink *Sou'wester*'s long-term future. While it's true that we currently lack funding and a diverse creative writing faculty—things outside of our immediate control—our university is home to a fantastic digital humanities center (IRIS) and our small department roster includes five dynamic African American literature scholars who offer a strong, vibrant African American literature curriculum. We are in the St. Louis Metro East area which has a rich literary history that includes the Black Arts

Movement; professor emeritus Eugene B. Redmond is the poet laureate of East St. Louis. Downtown Granite City, a former steel-making company town, is being revitalized; the Granite City Art and Design District, a consortium of creative project spaces, hosts a variety of exhibitions and a queer reading series.

Instead of continuing to try to do better with less, we've decided to try to do more with more. *Sou'wester* is currently on hiatus as we explore innovative, collaborative options—thinking far outside the conventional print journal box. We hope to move forward as a regionally-focused, inclusive, literature-promoting entity that better serves our diverse local community and promotes social justice.

To Consider

1 Regarding Vogrin's editing marks and comments on the manuscript, what do you notice? What do your observations make you think?

2 How does this case study compare to the Riddle case study? What do they have in common, and how are the editing approaches different?

3 What can you learn from this case study? How might this case study influence your editing in the future?

4 Choose one line from the interview—a line that feels magnetic and important, regardless of whether it inspires you or troubles you. Write about why you chose that line, and then "talk back" to it. In other words, respond to the line.

5 What questions do you have after reading this case study?

Maggie Smith

Poetry

Poet Maggie Smith has an extensive editing background, and has worked in children's and educational publishing, for trade publishers and university presses, and in consultation with poets on full manuscripts. When she edits a full-length poetry manuscript, she first reads the whole thing before making any editing marks. Her philosophy is succinct and worth remembering: "The better an editor does her job, the more invisible her work becomes."

Smith is the author of several books, including *Good Bones* and the national bestsellers *Goldenrod* and *Keep Moving: Notes on Loss, Creativity, and Change*. Her poems and essays have appeared in the *New York Times*, *The New Yorker*, *The Southern Review*, the *Guardian*, the *Paris Review*, *Tin House*, *APR*, the *Washington Post*, and *The Best American Poetry*. In 2016 her poem "Good Bones" went viral internationally and was called "the official poem of 2016" by PRI (Public Radio International). A freelance writer and editor, Smith is on the MFA faculty of the Naslund-Mann Graduate School of Writing and serves as an Editor-at-Large for the *Kenyon Review*. You can find her on social media @MaggieSmithPoet

Submitted Manuscript

The following poem was submitted by Gillian Cummings as part of a book manuscript. The original submission appears below.

"Ophelia Dreams of Sea Urchins"

Forever wed to water, she drifts far
into ocean, whose currents caress fair
creatures of the deep. Here, no harebell,
cowslip, gillyvor, no rosemary nor rue—
but seahorses curl tails less treacherously
than twined vines of nightshade, otters clutch
spiny prey with such innocence, they mother
their meal with lullabying, orphan uncertain
the hapless child. Mermaidlike, she cleaves
to blue, carves herself into waves that wash
memory away—forgetting is one blessing of
death's ongoing everness, to sleep unabashed—
here, the sting of brine, salt tangle of her hair,
whale song, rain's drum, a difference of air.

Maggie Smith's Editing Notes

At fourteen lines, it's sonnet-like in structure. It is part of a book manuscript I worked on with Gillian.

First I suggested changing "whose currents caress fair/creatures of the deep" to "fair creature of the deep," an extension of the description of Ophelia herself.

I also suggested removing the phrase "orphan uncertain/ the hapless child," as I preferred the movement from "lullabying" to "Mermaidlike," and the lovely alliteration (beginning M sounds), consonance (internal L sounds), and assonance (long I sounds) that can now live together on the line, uninterrupted by the deleted phrase.

Changing the lineation throughout the poem plays up—or plays down—the music, which is so lush and dense in Gillian's poems. For example, "no rosemary nor rue—but seahorses" on one line rather than split across two lines plays up the R and OR sounds. On the other hand, "twined/vines of nightshade" split across two lines now plays down the internal rhyme of twined/vines.

Finally, I changed some line breaks to play up tension and provide some breathing space at the end of lines. Breaking line nine at "into" provides suspense at the end of the line, so that the reader hangs for a moment before reading the rest of the sentence and answering the question, "Into what?" Breaking line ten at the long dash effectively doubles the pause of the dash.

Final Version

"Ophelia Dreams of Sea Urchins"

Forever wed to water, she drifts far
into ocean, fair creature of the deep.
Here, no harebell, cowslip, gillyvor,
no rosemary nor rue—but seahorses
curl tails less treacherously than twined
vines of nightshade, otters clutch spiny
prey with such innocence, they mother
their meal with lullabying. Mermaidlike,
she cleaves to blue, carves herself into
waves that wash memory away—
forgetting is one blessing of death's
ongoing everness, to sleep unabashed—
here, the sting of brine, salt tangle of her hair,
whale song, rain's drum, a difference of air.

Interview with Maggie Smith

On Beginning

I started out as an editor in children's publishing, reading the slush to find viable proposals and manuscripts, working with authors to develop the projects, editing throughout the production process, and writing jacket copy and marketing collateral. I went from trade publishing into educational publishing and worked in-house for large publishers for several years before striking out on my own as a freelance writer and editor. At that time I wrote and edited for educational publishers, working primarily on K-12 reading and language arts materials; copyedited and proofread for academics and university presses; and worked as an editor and consultant on poetry manuscripts. Today I continue to work on other writers' books as a freelance editor, and I mentor poets as an MFA faculty member at the Naslund-Mann Graduate School of Writing, but I primarily spend my time on my own writing projects. So I approach editorial work from a writer's perspective.

I find editorial work immensely satisfying. I like the feeling of sitting down with a piece of writing and identifying ways to make it stronger, clearer, and more resonant. There is instant gratification in finding an error and correcting it. Editors, and particularly proofreaders, are the last line of defense between an author and the reader. It's mortifying to have something published with errors, and so I take that job very seriously.

On Process

My process depends on the kind of work I'm doing. Copyediting a scholarly article or book requires a different approach than working on a manuscript for a poet. When working on a 350-page book, I do not do an initial cold read before beginning to mark up the pages;

I read carefully and mark as I go. When working on poetry, however, I read the whole manuscript through without making a mark, to get a sense of the writer's voice, tone, style, use of form, and thematic concerns. Then I go back through and begin to make suggestions. I typically edit electronically, using the Track Changes and Insert Comment functions in Microsoft Word—or the editing and commenting functions in Google Docs—to show the poet what I would recommend and to give some rationale for those recommendations.

My primary responsibility in the editing process is to the piece of writing itself. The suggestions I make on a poem are in service of the poem. However, when I insert queries and comments into a manuscript, my responsibility with that communication is to the writer. I also provide a manuscript consultation letter that summarizes my impressions of the manuscript and the kinds of changes I suggested. This is a document for the writer, and it gives me a chance to connect with the writer and say more than I could in the manuscript itself.

Communication and Collaboration with Writers

I know that writing and arranging a book are intuitive and personal processes, so I expect that some of what I suggest will resonate with the writer, but some of it will not. When I work on a book of poems, the most important thing is giving the poet options for how the poems might work, and for how they might work together in ways the poet may not have seen. I hope that my suggestions at the very least open a writer up to some new ideas for and about the project. It's so important to not only give sound advice as an editor but also to articulate it in a generous and respectful way. Opening oneself up to critique can be difficult, but I find that most writers crave detailed feedback and are open to suggestions if they understand the rationale and feel they—and their work—are being treated with respect.

Keys to Being a Good Editor

Do good work. Be thorough. Complete your work on time or, even better, before the deadline. Remember that an editor is there to do invisible work: the better an editor does her job, the more invisible her work becomes.

I remember one of my first editorial directors saying something about the three ideals in editorial work—fast, cheap, good—and how it's only really possible to get two out of three.

If it's good and cheap, it won't be fast. If it's good and fast, it won't be cheap. And if it's fast and cheap, it won't be very good.

Advice for Learning the Craft of Editing

Practice. The more you work on others' writing, the better you get at it. Hands-on experience is so important. Even though many of us edit our own work all the time, it's a completely different process to edit someone else's work. You have to maintain their style and voice. As a copyeditor, you want to make sure the work is clean and polished, but you don't want to overstep. As a literary editor, you can suggest more dramatic changes—removing a stanza from a poem, or cutting a poem from a book manuscript—but you still need to communicate that suggestion with respect and kindness, keeping in mind that you may have removed a poet's favorite line or favorite poem.

This seems obvious, but be professional, and be pleasant to work with. Even when facing tight deadlines or changing guidelines, keep your sense of humor and your perspective. Being cranky doesn't make the work better or faster or easier to do.

What Not to Do

Be wary of overstepping. Some pieces of writing may call for a dramatic overhaul, yes, but many need only a few small but impactful edits. An editor must remember that she is not rewriting a poem/sentence/paragraph/book to make the writing sound like her writing. The editor is there to polish the work and make it the best it can be, while also remaining true to the writer's voice and vision for the project.

To Consider

1 What are the benefits of reading an entire poetry manuscript before making any edits? Are there any drawbacks?

2 Practice, Smith says, is the key to becoming a good editor. What are some specific ways you can practice this "invisible art"?

3 Students often comment that poetry is one of the more difficult types of writing to edit, usually due to their lack of experience with the genre. Knowledge doesn't happen in a vacuum, and neither do poems. Research and make a list of five contemporary poetry collections you'd like to read, and five more from before 1950. Read them, share them, talk about them.

4 Reread the original and published versions of Gillian Cummings's "Ophelia Dreams of Sea Urchins." What do you notice in terms of sound, imagery, or line breaks? How has the editing changed the work? Would you make similar edits? Why/why not?

5 If you've never written a poem, now's the time. Find inspiration at websites like poems.com or www.poetryfoundation.org. Understanding a genre from the inside-out is a great step for the novice who wants to edit thoughtfully and with empathy.

Mark Doten

Novel Excerpt

Mark Doten is the executive editor of Soho Press in Manhattan, where he champions a wide variety of writers. Doten does not dictate changes to writers; his process is more collaborative. In an editing nutshell: "Don't pressure an author to make choices they aren't comfortable with."

Doten acquired and edited Brandon Hobson's novel, *Where the Dead Sit Talking*, and the following edited excerpt shows Doten and Hobson in conversation about suggested changes to the novel manuscript. It's a lighter edit, Doten says, and he was involved in all stages of the book's publication.The novel went on to become a National Book Award finalist in 2018.

(Editors' Note: Because these suggested edits didn't significantly change the text, we omitted the final, published version from this Case Study. What follows is the submitted version, providing a look at a more global manuscript edit.)

Submitted Manuscript with Editing Marks

I never had many friends. In Cherokee County, I knew a boy named Monfiori who lived in the neighborhood. He was pale-skinned and thin with wiry hair. Everyone at school hated him, but for a while he was my only companion. He ate cockroaches for a dollar and huffed paint behind the woodshop building. He smoked cigarettes in my bedroom despite my weak lungs and my coughing. My mother was worried people would think I was a troublemaker for being friends with him.

> Was wondering about placement of this section with Monfiori? Is it working at this point in the book or should it be placed earlier?

"We're like hemophiliac brothers," Monfiori said. "They tell us don't bleed, don't bleed, but we're dying anyway. They don't know anything."

"I'm not a hemophiliac," I told him.

Somehow he didn't believe me. He'd made comments about the burn marks on my face, that I needed to watch out in case they ever bled me to death.

"That'll never happen," I told him. "They're scars."

He refused to believe me. He played jazz on a toy trumpet. "Variations on Monk in C," his own creation, this arrangement—or so he claimed. "Psychedelic funk," he called it. We drank cheap vodka in his basement, and I played drums on upside down buckets. I liked being at his house because I could drink and smoke over there without anyone knowing.

> Is this an actual song? I can't find any record of it and song names would be placed in quotes, not italics. If this is not an actual song but the name he gave the song he played on the toy trumpet then it doesn't need to be capped. And what is "Psychedelic Funk," the name of the type of music he played? If so, funk does not need to be capitalized.

"My mom has jazz records," I told him. "She listens to them on nights she wants to be left alone."

"She'll be alone soon enough when you die," he said.

Monfiori said we were both dying. "Might as well poison ourselves," he said. "At least that way we'll die in our sleep." He'd already gotten two blood transfusions. He had bruises and moles all over his body. I saw the moles on his cheek and neck. His hair

> This is a fictional song title Monfiori made up—Monk being a reference to Thelonius Monk and C being the key. I added quotes.--Brandon

hung in his eyes and always looked unkempt, but I liked it. He was probably the ugliest boy in our school, and maybe the meanest.

One time in his basement we smoked a joint and he told me he was going to set the school on fire. "We'll watch the whole place go up in flames," he said. "I'll send smoke signals to the Indians. Fuck the police and everyone else."

Monfiori and I had to do twenty hours of community service for stealing guitar strings from the music store downtown. We were going to use them to tie the spokes and chain of his brother's bicycle so that he would crash. Monfiori's mom and aunt caught us later in his backyard as we were tying the strings to the spokes. They made us return the packages of guitar strings to the music store. The owner wanted to press charges and we had to go to juvenile court.

> It's not quite clear how they were caught or by whom; seems very odd that they'd be arrested for shoplifting once they'd already made it home and in any case "caught" doesn't seem like the right word since it leads one to think of them being interrupted in the act but in fact they'd already stolen the string and made it home. . .unless they what they were caught doing was tying the bike spokes with the strings, but again, who caught them? More explicit wording might make this scenario easier to imagine.

"My son's not a bad kid," my mother kept telling everyone.

That same winter I fell ill with a stomach virus and my asthma flared up. The breathing machine they had me use was loud enough to hear throughout the house. At night the dogs next door kept me awake with their barking. They belonged to our neighbors, who were an old couple, immigrants from Poland. Their names were Milosz and Gertrude. They brought me soup and crackers and a dessert called *faworki*, which they said was known as angel wings.

"They're for good luck," Gertrude told me. "It's a Polish specialty."

My mother and Gertrude became close. They talked about bread and sausages and red wine. Milosz made paper airplanes for me. From my bed, in my sickness, I watched him pull up a chair. He folded a piece of paper into an airplane and tossed it across the room.

"I had a son once," Milosz told me. "My wife and I lost him. He was about your age."

He stared into the floor. He seemed to be searching for the right words. We could hear my mother and Gertrude laughing in the next room.

"His name was Aleksander," he said. "He liked to play the piano."

I could see the lines in his forehead, the loose skin of his jowls.

"My son, my son," he said.

He folded another piece of paper. I watched his fingers move, all bone and skin. He concentrated on each fold, creasing it, holding it up to the light to make sure he got it right. He folded the paper into a bird and handed it to me.

"You can name it anything you want," he said.

"Aleksander," I said.

I held the paper bird. I noticed Milosz's hands were trembling.

"Aleksander it is," he said. He stared into the floor.

Those days I was sick I would often see a male cardinal appear on the branch outside my window. One morning I opened the window and he flew in. He was such a beautiful bird. He flew wildly around my room. He glided from desk to bedpost, from bookshelf to lampshade. His wings were red like velvet. He was proud but silent. He seemed to be attentive to some inner presence, as if he had a clear point to make as he strutted across the windowsill. Once, he spread his wings proudly for me. This was his own show, a brief abandonment of the natural world, his own strange fantasy. The last time I saw him, that winter day I was ill, he flew in and shook the frost from his body. I let him eat sugar from my hand. In the pale light of my bedroom, in one final, cool gesture of farewell, he cocked his head to look at me, then flew out the window.

For several weeks Milosz continued to bring me paper birds made from colored construction paper. I hung them with string from my ceiling so that they twirled constantly. There were red birds, blue birds, yellow birds, purple birds. Monfiori didn't like them. "Can we set them on fire?" he asked.

"No."

"Aren't you too old for this? Look at this place."

He challenged my integrity. He dared me to cut myself and bleed. I challenged him back and he laughed it off. One Friday I stayed the night at his house. We drank his mother's vodka until late. I fell asleep on the floor in his basement and woke up at some point in the middle of the night, feeling sick. I found him sitting in the corner of the room, watching me.

"What is it?" I asked.

He mumbled something.

"What's wrong with you?" I said.

"We're both dying," he said. "We'll die together."

I was sick the whole next day. In my room, Milosz sipped wine and told me stories about a boy who kept birds to fend off devils. "The birds protected him," he said. "They changed colors and held healing powers, like tiny gods or angels. They showed courage. They taught the boy to believe in himself."

Milosz wheezed and coughed. I coughed, too. His glass of red wine seemed to glow in the dim room. The paper birds twirled above our heads.

One night I woke to something knocking at my window. I sat up in bed, pulled back the curtain but saw nothing. Outside, the wind was blowing. It was a tree branch, I told myself, and went back to sleep.

Later I dreamed of the cardinal at my window. The cardinal spread his wings, glowing red in the night.

Weeks passed and Monfiori left my life as quickly as he'd entered. I saw him for the last time later that winter. We sat in his basement drinking cheap vodka and smoking cigarettes. I watched him wrestle his little brother to the floor and punch him in the chest until the boy started crying and ran out of the room.

"You need to stop being mean," I told him.

"I'm not," he said. "We're dying, so what does it matter?"

He turned on the strobe light. We stayed up late in the night listening to some sort of death metal, all screams and guitar. I remember slamming my body into the wall. I remember lying on the floor and pulling a blanket over myself.

I'm convinced he tried to poison me in my sleep. The next morning they found me unresponsive. I don't remember being carried out of the house, the ambulance ride, or anything else. I woke up in a hospital bed on the third floor of Southwest Central Hospital, where they watched me for several days. There, my mother kept telling the nurses I wasn't a bad kid. They fed me tapioca pudding. They helped me out of bed and tried to talk to me, but I wanted to be left alone. I watched cartoons and old movies on TV.

"He's a quiet kid," one of the nurses told my mother. "He never talks."

When I returned home, the first people who came to see me were Milosz and Gertrude. They brought me angel wings. We drank tea and listened to old records on the antique record player. I mostly kept to myself in my bedroom.

My mother said Monfiori had tried to hang himself and they took him away. He wouldn't be coming back for a while.

"That boy is nothing like my son," my mother told Milosz and Gertrude. "He was trouble, it's so sad," she said.

They all agreed I was nothing like him.

"My son is very happy," my mother kept saying.

*   *   *

At the Troutts, we usually ate dinner around six in the evening. Rosemary ate alone in her room and nobody questioned it. I saw it as some sort of healing mechanism for her that required no explanation. Maybe the conversation had been exhausted. Maybe they gave up. Every night around ten, Harold came upstairs from the basement and watched the evening news before he went upstairs to bed. Agnes always sat in the same recliner in the living room, reading the bible or some book on spirituality.

Since the night Rosemary had given me the books, I became more and more drawn to her. As the only Indians around, we shared a culture and blood unknown to the others. We were like branches intertwined from the same tree, the same root, reaching out toward the sky to the unknown. I felt drawn to her as a brother is to a lost sister, nothing more. Maybe I felt too strongly. I see now that I tended to get attached easily, but at the time I felt it was necessary to be near her, watch her, even protect her if I needed to. I kept all this to myself.

George, however, became unbearable with all his eccentricities. He paced, muttered to himself, continually asked me questions about where I came from. Nights he continued to make explosion noises with his mouth, keeping me awake. He stayed in his room, writing notes in a notebook and memorizing the birthdates of rock stars. One afternoon after school he wanted me to tell him about the Cherokees, so I told him about the Trail of Tears, which he was learning about in his Oklahoma History class. I spoke the words of a song one of my mother's boyfriends had taught me, written many years ago by some unknown Cherokee man:

> I am a proud Cherokee, don't take away my land.
> Don't take away my land, this here is Cherokee land.
> I'm a proud Cherokee, don't take away my land,
> You mean old white man.

> I got a bottle full of wine, some rum and whiskey too.
> I'm a-gonna get drunk on rum and whiskey, too.
> I'm a-gonna get drunk, and I'll show you what I'll do,
> You mean old white man.

> When your train comes to town, you better go away.
> You better go away, you took my land away.
> I'm a-gonna get drunk, you better go away,
> You mean old white man.

Song lyrics, check if rights needed

I made up these lyrics, so no rights needed.--Brandon

George wrote the lyrics in his notebook. When he was finished he asked what key it was in. "It's like a folk song?" he asked. "Is it played on acoustic guitar?"

"I think so. I don't know."

"Sounds like a folk song," he said.

He set the notebook down and looked up to the ceiling, then back to the floor. "Rosemary's in the woods with some guy," he said.

I sat up in bed. "In the woods?"

"She goes there to draw. She draws in the woods."

"But with a guy?"

"She draws naked people," he said. "I've seen her drawings. She draws naked men and women. Do you want to see them? I know where they are in her room."

"Why do they go to the woods?" I asked.

He pulled on his lower lip, staring at the floor.

"George," I said.

"To draw, to draw," he said.

I went downstairs and put on my coat. As I walked by the kitchen window I saw Rosemary and a boy standing outside in the backyard. She was holding her large sketchbook and they were talking. I stood there watching them for a moment. Rosemary was saying something. The boy laughed and then Rosemary laughed. Then they started to walk toward the woods.

Interview with Mark Doten

On Beginnings

I was pursuing a fiction MFA in New York City when I got a half-time gig as assistant at a small literary agency. From there I moved to Soho Press as managing editor. I've been at Soho for thirteen years, but was only managing editor a short while (a managing editor, in general, does not edit books, but is in charge of keeping production schedules on track and moving manuscripts through the steps that transform a lowly Word doc into the lovely final book you hold in your hands at the bookstore). I am not a great one with schedules, but luckily for all involved, my job shifted from managing editor to being an acquiring editor with a focus on literary fiction. The first book I edited on my own was *Luminarium* by Alex Shakar, which was a good one to start with, because it is a massive, complex book that blends real and virtual experiences in interesting ways, and the author was very open to edits, while also being willing to defend his choices where he felt my suggestions were wrong for the book. It was a very open, free-flowing editorial process, and an ideal learning experience for how editor and author can dig in, debate, and discuss things, from a single comma to global structural changes. That book got good year-end attention and won the LA Times novel prize, so it was a little like walking into the casino and winning a decent jackpot on your first pull. One's books as an editor do not, of course, all perform like that, but it didn't matter, I was already hooked on the job.

On Process

It varies. If I'm reading a submission that I'm likely to offer on, I'll write a few notes to myself as I go. This is useful for talking about the book at an editorial meeting (where you would likely talk about what edits you envision for the book) and also for that initial phone conversation with the author. The big question in terms of process is whether a book has a two-stage edit or if I put in all the comments and edits at the same time. The two-stage edit can be useful if there are larger structural issues to address—if there is substantial rewriting to be done, then it often is best to do that first, so you're not line-editing material that's going to change later. If there are these larger changes to be made, I would have discussed with the author prior to finalizing the offer for the book.

Keys to Being a Good Editor

One key: the ability to read a manuscript and develop a feel for how its various formal elements work, the effects these choices create. Is the story fragmented and elliptical, or is it told in a "straightforward," chronological fashion? What is on the page, and what does the author leave out? Why does the author use short sentences in chapter one and long run-ons in others? Why does the author provide a flurry of specific details on page seven, when pages eight and nine are abstracted and generalized? How does the author establish the "voice" or "voices" of a novel, and when does the author break with these voices? These are only a few of the countless formal choices we might see in a book. None of these have a clear, unequivocal, singular effect—different readers will encounter them in different ways. The author will have made many of these decisions intuitively, without a specific signification in mind. But you, as editor, should have a working sense of the constellations of possible effects produced by the author's formal choices. And you should have a sense of when a particular formal element of the book (the flurry of specific details mentioned above) works, and when you feel it doesn't work. Then you have to communicate all that to the author, and have a conversation about it. There is no inherent value to any of these formal choices. Short chapters are not "better" than long chapters. The question is always: what effects do they create in a given manuscript? Are they the strongest choices for the book? Most novels have thousands or tens of thousands of sentences. I've published many of those. I've also published a one-sentence novel, Mike McCormack's *Solar Bones*. Both forms can be great.

Another key is being a good salesperson. While publicity and marketing do most of the public-facing selling, the editor represents and talks about the book over and over. So you start to develop your pitch, your way of discussing it, the first time you bring it up at ed meeting. And you continue to develop and improve your ability to talk about the book for the next year or two, in the run-up to pub: with in-house marketing and publicity, at sales meetings for national and regional sales reps, at lunches or Zooms with librarians and booksellers, and so on. Your ability to communicate why this book is so amazingly exciting is an important part of the book's future.

Advice for Learning the Craft of Editing

To the extent possible, edit books that you are passionate about. There is nothing better than that feeling of focused engagement when closely reading, thinking about, and commenting on a book you love. If you don't get that feeling at least some of the time, you'll burn out.

On Diversity, Representation, and Equity in Editing

Editors have a serious responsibility here. The choices we make as editors – what we choose to bring to ed meeting, and then to push for at sales meetings, and later to talk up in all the various places editors talk things up – have material effects both for individual authors and for the overall publishing landscape. I'm white; many authors I edit are not. It is part of my job to actively seek out and consider work from writers of color. Because much of the fiction I publish is unconventional in one way or another, I feel an extra responsibility to writers of color doing the weird stuff. The publishing world can be unfriendly to work that pushes on formal boundaries, and that can be doubly so for writers of color. You hear this all the time from writers of color: how the publishing world wants to put them in a box, wants them to do a certain type of story that is familiar and comfortable. And of course writers of color should have the same freedom that white people have to write whatever weird stuff they want to. Some of the most successful novels I've worked on have been formally unconventional works by writers of color. I think of Brandon Hobson's *Where the Dead Sit Talking*, which tells the story of a fifteen-year-old Cherokee boy in foster care, and is vibrating with strange energies, seeming to move into an almost dream-like space at moments. Or Gina Apostol's *Insurrecto*, which stacks multiple competing realities as it explores the nature of art and memory and the atrocities committed by the US during the Philippine-American War; or the nested stories and shifting identities in Ernesto Mestre-Reed's *Sacrificio*, about a band of young, HIV-positive revolutionaries in 1990s Cuba.

These are all incredibly cool books, amazingly written, and they made money and got strong reviews. So while some people on the sales side of publishing may have in their mind the platonic ideal of a "book club book" by a writer of color, it's always been true that it's the strange stuff that we remember. *Invisible Man*, *Beloved*, *The Woman Warrior*, or a more recent novel like Justin Torres's *We the Animals*—all of them are deeply strange and unconventional books, and it's because of this that they are classics. It is precisely through messing with form that these authors create works that are so capacious and provoking. The characters in these books, the stories in these books, could not exist in a more conventional form. They would be other, and less interesting, characters and stories.

Beyond this, support the hiring of editors who are not white.

What Not to Do

Don't pressure an author to make choices they aren't comfortable with. If there is disagreement, you can make the case for a particular edit, but you have to let it go if the author disagrees. It's their book.

To Consider

1　Pick a novel or story collection you've read before. (This may work best for one that you thought needed improvement.) Write a one-page editorial letter detailing the changes you'd make before publishing the book.

2　Using that same book, study how it's constructed. Doten says that editors "develop a feel for how [a manuscript's] various formal elements work, the effects these choices create. Is the story fragmented and elliptical, or is it told in a 'straightforward,' chronological fashion? What is on the page, and what does the author leave out?" Using those questions as a starting point, make notes that take in both the big picture and the details.

3　How do biases and backgrounds play a role in editing? How can editors be better advocates for a wider representation of writers and voices in book publishing?

4　Doten gave *Where the Dead Sit Talking* a lighter edit. In what ways might you choose to use a "less is more" approach to editing? Why?

5　In this interview, Doten mentions numerous books he's worked on or admires. Pick one that is unfamiliar to you and research the book and the author. See if you can learn about the book's editorial process. (Acknowledgements inside the book or author interviews are good starting points.) Better yet: read one or more from cover to cover.

Student Examples

Universities are not nimble institutions. Arriving at a decision typically involves a long process that includes researching what "peer and aspirant" universities are doing about the issue at hand. "Aspirant" is code for institutions the university wants to someday be like; "peer" is code for institutions that the university thinks it is currently like.

All the previous case studies have featured seasoned professional editors. You might consider those "aspirant models." The next two case studies feature emerging editors, undergraduate students in a literary editing class. Since this book is primarily designed to be a textbook for such classes, let's call these "peer models."

Why include peer models? Two reasons. First, studying peer models can help you set expectations for your own editing work. Secondly, if a book is for students, it should include student voices—especially because the idea for this book came from a student.

That student was Grace Dillow. *Wouldn't it be great*, she said during a visit to office hours one day, *if we could see how editors work with writers on their manuscripts?* Her idea gave rise to these case studies, and eventually this book. It's fitting, then, for us to look at her own work as an editor.

Grace Dillow worked on Butler's undergraduate literary magazine, *Manuscripts*, and held the position of Editing Chair before graduating in 2017. She edited the following story as well as other submissions that appeared in the magazine.

Grace Dillow

Short Fiction (Student Example)

Submitted Manuscript with Editing Marks

The following story was submitted by Katherine Shelton to *Manuscripts*, which published the final version.

"Stained"

The large conference room, normally housing lectures, had been colonized by unfamiliar persons. Volunteers checked donors in and offered battered, laminated pages detailing any juvenile or scientific question on the process of blood donation. tThe recovery center was at a desk on the opposite wall, furnished with granola bars, cookies, and enough bottled water to shorten the planet's life expectancy by a few years. Nurses scurried <u>to and fro,</u>: retrieving necessaries at a communal table in the center of the room, wiping and sticking donors at gurneys, assessing possible donors behind portable walls, and repeating the process.

This particular room and setup was familiar enough for Ms. Nuja. She had travelled around ~~locale to locale~~site to site within the city, seeing so much that all the individual portraits morphed into a broad ~~murale~~mural. It hung like a tapestry in the back of her mind and there she let it expand, each addition seeming smaller in its accumulated growth until the majesty was lost entirely.

> I love this metaphor! I think maybe it would be a little clearer though if you said "seeing so many people that the individual portraits morphed into a broad mural"

A young man, perhaps an older boy, practically skipped into the room. It was not only his pink shoelaces that gave off a distinct air of femininity. Nuja looked to the other nurses, who gave a collective, small frown. This group, Nuja acknowledged with a groan, disliked turning people away. She, however, was seasoned; the worst case scenario was that the stranger walked away with all of his blood.

Still, even people at the front desk who got a glimpse of his bony hands were polite and committed to procedure. Nuja would do the same.

"Would you like a free T-shirt?" the acne-ridden volunteer chirped.

"Oh!" the young man was taken aback by the honor, "No, thank you very much, m̶Miss! I don't need it."

The girl took another look over the missing buttons in his shirt. "I think we have your size, though."

"You're so nice," ~~he spoke like melting butter~~his voice was like melting butter, and his copper eyes ~~even~~seemed to deepen, "But no, I don't need it. Thank you."

Nuja approached the conversing pair and addressed the boy, "First time donor?"

"No, m̶Miss," he drew his too-long sleeves back over his jutting elbows before immediately pulling his sleeves back down again.

Ms. Nuja raised her eyebrows in response. Although she did not appear old in a physical sense, her gentility had long been squelched from her in an effort to be taken seriously. As a result, strangers generally called her "m̶Ma'am" over "m̶Miss." It

> The detail of his fidgeting is great here. I can see how nervous he is.

made her feel young, this boy addressing her in such a way. Their age difference prevented any romantic stirrings, but she was flattered ideologically. Only now was she beginning to feel sorry for the emaciated, presumably gay boy. His eagerness buzzed off of his skin. "Well, you can follow me back when you're ready."

"I'm ready now, if you don't mind, ~~m~~Miss. Not to rush you! I only meant I could go if you would rather not wait around." He looked horrified with his tongue-tied state, his giddiness draining from him. "Or maybe you'd rather have a break. I'm sorry, just do whatever you want."

Ms. Nuja stared at him a moment, trying to discern if she believed he was spineless or simply too polite. But in the end, it made little difference. "Come on," she said, and led him back behind a portable wall she had helped set up earlier that day. On the other side sat two chairs and a computer with a list of reasons why he could not donate. She could think of a couple reasons more than the automated system. For example, a grinning boy who wore thin clothes in the winter had no business giving anything away.

> I love this – it evokes such sympathy.

Still, Nuja sat down in her chair and began the online survey. "I'm going to have to ask you a few questions. If you've donated before, a lot of this should be in our system anyway, but we want to keep everything up to date." She glanced up at him, his sleeves falling down past his hands, his weight teetering between his feet as he bashfully scanned the floor. "You can sit," she offered.

"I may?" his blistered lips smiled a touch too widely, and started to bleed a little. "~~Oh, of course, t~~Thank you, ~~m~~Miss."

The power of the word "~~m~~Miss" was starting ~~to turn on her~~to wane. "Please, call me Fola. Or Ms. Nuja." She cut him off before he could apologize, "First, your name?"

"Katurian P. Napels."

Nuja suppressed a smile. It was always a pleasure to find others in the "say that again?"-name category. "Spell that for me?"

He obeyed, and additionally set his ID on the table. From this, she gathered that he had recently turned 18.

"Happy belated birthday, Katurian."

"Thank you, Miss Fola Nuja."

Most of the general information was fine. He seemed to hesitate over an address before he simply pointed to the one on his identification. Nuja ~~hesitated~~paused slightly ~~at~~over his height and weight, an irrational guilt resonating in her gut.

Katurian scratched the back of his head knowingly, ruffling up his already disheveled~~messy~~, brown bowl-cut. "I guess I'm a little underweight . . ."

That was an understatement. His skin appeared to struggle in stretching over his bones. "Yes. I'm afraid this could be a problem."

"Why, exactly?" he leaned forward in his chair, his wide eyes looking all the larger.

Again, Nuja hesitated. "For your ~~safety~~own wellbeing."

Katurian nodded slowly, "Is that the only reason?"

"Isn't that reason enough?"

Katurian smiled, that dab of blood from his lips smearing slightly over his crooked teeth. "Next question?"

Nuja sighed, sounding almost sympathetic. "I'm afraid there's no need. I'm not legally allowed to put you in harm's way, it goes against the entire purpose."

Katurian's soft eyes darkened in an instant. "No, ~~m~~Miss, I *insist*."

He did nothing actively threatening, but at the very least, Nuja no longer believed he was a pushover. He did not look eager to fight, per se, but she caught sight of a reservoir of power inside of this boy. It ~~took~~knocked her off her game. "Katurian, I could lose my job if I don't turn you away at this point."

His jaw twitched strangely, all nuances of which were visible in his starved face. "I want to save a life."

"Save yours."

His entire demeanor greyed. They stared at one another in complete disillusionment. At last, he stood, and Nuja sat up a bit straighter. She picked up his ID and reached out to return it to him. The barrel of a gun was positioned directly in front of her left eye. Katurian cocked the small pistol.

"I'm terribly sorry," his voice wavered, but his hand did not. "I really <u>must</u> insist we go through with this, ~~m~~Miss."

* * *

She did not ask why this was so important. She did not cry for help. She was not going to argue or barter. She was going to get through this nightmare as briskly as possible. Her life was the goal, and so she was perfectly obedient, even if she trembled.

They got through health history questions without any problems. Midway through, Katurian put his gun back in his pocket, under the too-long shirt. He sat back in his chair, drawing his knees to his chest. He was ~~such~~just a child, which terrified her to her core.

"Have you had homosexual intercourse?" Nuja queried softly.

Katurian frowned. "Consenting or not?"

"It doesn't matter."

The boy flinched. "Seems like it should matter."

Nuja clicked her tongue indifferently, "I'll just say no. That one is left over from the AIDS scare anyway."

After completing a few more questions and lying about his weight, Nuja paused. Adrenaline prevented exhaustion, but she was still perplexed into idleness.

"What's wrong?" Katurian asked.

She looked at him flatly and whispered, "Aside from my life being threatened?"

He bit his lip. "I'm really sorry about that. But you were gonna make me leave."

"I can't just start draining your blood out there. You're obviously ineligible. And I'm not sure how much is safe to take from you."

Katurian drummed his fingers on his knees anxiously. "Well, I can help you ~~w~~with the last one. You're going to take ~~all of it out~~it all."

Nuja momentarily forgot how to breathe. "You're making me murder you?"

"But I don't want you to get in trouble or anything. Maybe you could bring the gurney back here, say I'm embarrassed but wanna ~~give what I can~~donate? I'll write a

> I'm a little hesitant here. I feel like there should be another back and forth here before Nuja says this line because I feel like she wouldn't be that clear in her thinking right off the bat. I like the "forgot how to breathe" part though and it's a great instance of panic.

note to let everyone know I'm okay with this, that I'm making you. Sign it and everything. Will that work?"

"You're making me murder you."

Katurian's smile was patient. "If you don't mind, ~~M~~miss, I would appreciate it. I *was* going to just do it the old-fashioned way, with razorblades. Only that felt like a terrible waste."

> **What if Nuja commented on the "if you don't mind" part." That way we could get a little more reaction/emotion with this part.**

"Katurian. . ." She didn't think to wonder why he wouldn't use the gun in his pocket.

"Can you imagine?" His words bounced. "All that blood just. . . wasted. I have enough iron and I'm not sick."

"You *are* sick," Ms. Nuja hissed.

Katurian pouted. "Not in a way that anyone else will catch."

"You need help," Nuja insisted with quiet, vicious urgency, "Just go home and talk to your parents—"

> **I think it might be more powerful if you say "despite his sadness" or "despite the tragedy behind it" or something – just a little more specific.**

He looked sad, but not for himself, for Nuja. "I can't do that. You're kind of overestimating me, ~~m~~Miss. Nobody can stand to be near me, especially the people who had to have me." He offered his best smile. It was gorgeous despite everything. "Can we please just do this? It'll be over before you know it, promise."

"I'll take you," she promised, "-to someone who can help you."

"*You're* going to help me."

> **Can you think of a different way of phrasing this since you used it a few pages up to describe Katurian? Something to support the next phrase – show her anger.**

They stared at one another. He reached a hand past his loose shirt and into his pocket. Her entire demeanor greyed. She would not let him point a gun at her again.

"Fine," she conceded. "I'll do it."

*   *   *

Just beyond her and Katurian's walled off corner of the room, everything ran smoothly. Two large, open, trusting entrances, free gifts as one entered and as one exited. Not one moment did anyone check security. Not one camera in this massive room. All smiles and laughs and jokes out there. ~~She~~Nuja wanted to vomit.

> **There's a little gap here. Maybe end the last break with "and she headed out" or begin this line with something about her coming out into the wide space since she is kind of locked in her own world with Katurian behind that very thin wall.**

Instead, ~~Ms. Nuja~~she kicked up the locks on the wheels of a gurney and proceeded to push it back behind the fake wall. When she returned to the main, open area, another nurse approached her.

"What's going on?"

Nuja could only muster a head shake as she proceeded to transport the rest of her necessary materials.

Apparently, she reeked of trauma. The nurse grabbed her arm. "What is going on? Should I. . ." She faltered, trying to read Nuja's expression, "~~D~~do I need to call someone?"

Nuja nodded, simplicity lightening her slowly and then ferociously. She whispered, "911. Be subtle. He's armed." Nuja broke away from her grasp.

"What are you doing? Don't go back!"

> **Should she be smiling here? Or should it be some other emotion conveyed in her expression?**

"If I don't, he'll come out here." There was a certainty that was frightening and convincing in Nuja's smile. "Just trust me."

*   *   *

Nuja pushed back ~~his~~Katurian's sleeve and turned his forearm in her small hands, looking for the perfect vein. Instead, she found several bruises and scars. They decorated his skin like an abstract painting. She stared breathlessly.

Katurian apologized in his inflection, "My left arm is just as bad." He fidgeted uncomfortably, as if she was staring at his naked form. "Should I flex or something? Would that make it easier to find?"

"No, it's alright," Nuja assured him, her hands suddenly gentler, that breath rushing out of her all at once. "There's not much place for them to hide, after all."

After checking that he had no applicable allergies, she wiped his inner arm clean. As she prepared the needle, she habitually~~-~~ recited, "I'm sorry, this might leave a mark." Katurian laughed, which brought her back to the present. Caught somewhere between a sob and a chortle, she punctured him, and screwed the proper tubing together.

Katurian gulped, transfixed by the image of his blood coursing out of him. "Jeez, that's kinda scary looking."

Nuja pulled up a chair beside him. "It would have been scarier with a razor blade."

Katurian nodded distantly, gaping at the artificial artery that extended out of him, pooling very cleanly and distantly from him.

The two sat in silence for a long time. The flow of blood began to slow, and before she could stop herself, she told him that opening and closing his fist would help speed up the process. Naturally, he obeyed, and within five minutes, he had given a pint.

"Guess my blood is dying to get out," he joked.

"Mmhm," Nuja responded humorlessly, clamping the tubing as she replaced this bag with a new one.

"A quarter of the way through, right? Something like that?"

"Yes, Mr. Napels."

Katurian did not take particularly well to being addressed so formally. He ravenously pumped his hand in and out of a fist.

"I'm awful sorry, Miss Fola Nuja." ⸳⸳⸳⸳⸳⸳⸳⸳⸳⸳⸳⸳⸳⸳⸳⸳⸳⸳⸳⸳⸳⸳⸳⸳⸳⸳⸳⸳⸳⸳⸳⸳⸳⸳⸳⸳⸳⸳

> This is the first time that Katurian actually calls her by her name after she gets irritated by all the misses. Maybe that can be worked in earlier or she can mention it again after a while since she is such a strong character.

She blinked. "What for?"

"You didn't ask to get mixed up in this. I probably ruined your whole day."

Her eyes locked on him. Katurian sheepishly shrugged and leaned his head back. "Never been dizzy sitting down before. It's weird."

Her gaze was merciless. He silenced himself for good under its pressure. His hand moved more and more slowly, until it merely unfurled.

The realization leaked into Nuja's consciousness like a steadily sinking lifeboat. Why would Katurian use razor blades if he had a working gun? Did he not have a working gun? What had he been threatening her with? Did he have no real ammunition with which to harm her after all? Had she been tricked?

It was too late. His eyelids drifted shut and his breathing slowed. Nuja jumped to her feet, clamping the tube, preventing any more blood from escaping.

By this point, ~~cops~~police arrived on the scene.

"No!" Nuja shrieked, standing in front of the battered, unconscious boy, "I changed my mind! I don't need you, I need an ambulance!" She scooped up the blood bags and placed

I feel like there should be some sort of resolution here. I want to know if he died or not, if he made it to the hospital, what Nuja's response to his death is – something like that. I just feel like it ends too quickly here. Do they rush him away and she's left standing, waiting to hear what will happen or does she look for the gun and find it's a toy? Just some suggestions to consider!

them on top of Katurian. "Put it back! It's his, I'll explain it all later, *just put it back in his little body right now!*"

Final Version

"Stained"

The large conference room, normally housing lectures, had been colonized by unfamiliar persons. Volunteers checked donors in and offered battered, laminated pages detailing any juvenile or scientific question on the process of blood donation. The recovery center was at a desk on the opposite wall, furnished with granola bars, cookies, and enough bottled water to shorten the planet's life expectancy by a few years. Nurses scurried to and fro, retrieving necessaries at a communal table in the center of the room, wiping and sticking donors at gurneys, assessing possible donors behind portable walls, and repeating the process.

This particular room and setup was familiar enough for Ms. Nuja. She had travelled around site to site within the city, seeing so much that all the individual portraits morphed into a broad mural. It hung like a tapestry in the back of her mind and there she let it expand, each addition seeming smaller in its accumulated growth until the majesty was lost entirely.

A young man, perhaps an older boy, practically skipped into the room. It was not only his pink shoelaces that gave off a distinct air of femininity. The other nurses gave a collective, small frown. This group, Nuja acknowledged with a groan, disliked turning people away. She, however, was seasoned; the worst case scenario was that the stranger walked away with all of his blood.

Still, even people at the front desk who got a glimpse of his bony hands were polite and committed to procedure. Nuja would do the same.

"Would you like a free T-shirt?" the acne-ridden volunteer chirped.

"Oh!" The young man was taken aback by the honor, "No, thank you very much, Miss! I don't need it."

The girl took another look over the missing buttons in his shirt. "I think we have your size, though."

"You're so nice," his voice was like melting butter, "But no, I won't need it."

Nuja approached the conversing pair and addressed the boy, "First time donor?"

"Yes, Miss," he drew his too-long sleeves back over his jutting elbows before immediately pulling his sleeves back down again.

Ms. Nuja raised her eyebrows in response. Gentility had long been squelched from her in an effort to be taken seriously, resulting in strangers typically calling her "ma'am" over "Miss." She was flattered by this boy's deviance from the norm— ideologically flattered, not romantically. Only now was she beginning to feel sorry for the emaciated, presumably gay boy. His eagerness buzzed off of his skin. "Well, you can follow me back when you're ready."

"I'm ready now, if you don't mind, Miss. Not to rush you! I only meant I could go if you would rather not wait." He looked horrified with his tongue-tied state, his giddiness draining from him. "Or maybe you'd rather have a break. I'm sorry, just do whatever you want."

Ms. Nuja stared at him a moment, trying to discern if she believed he was spineless or simply too polite. But in the end, it made little difference. "Come on," she said, and led him back behind a portable wall she had helped set up earlier that day. On the other side sat two chairs and a computer with a list of reasons why he could not donate. She could think of a couple reasons more than the automated system. For example, a grinning boy who wore thin clothes in the winter had no business giving anything away.

Still, Nuja sat down in her chair and began the online survey. "I'm going to have to ask you a few questions." She glanced up at him, his weight teetering between his feet as he bashfully scanned the floor. "You can sit," she offered.

"I may?" his blistered lips smiled a touch too widely, and started to bleed a little. "Thank you, Miss."

The power of the word "Miss" started to nauseate her. "Please, call me Fola. Or Ms. Nuja." She cut him off before he could apologize, "First, your name?"

"Katurian P. Napels."

Nuja suppressed a smile. It was always a pleasure to find others in the "say that again?"-name category. "Spell that for me?"

He obeyed, and additionally set his ID on the table. From this, she gathered that he had recently turned 18.

"Happy belated birthday, Katurian."

"Thank you, Miss Fola Nuja."

Most of the general information was fine. He seemed to hesitate over an address before he simply pointed to the one on his identification. Nuja paused over his height and weight, an irrational guilt resonating in her gut.

Katurian scratched the back of his head knowingly, ruffling up his already messy, brown bowl-cut. "I guess I'm a little underweight . . ."

That was an understatement. His skin appeared to struggle in stretching over his bones. "Yes. I'm afraid this could be a problem."

"Why, exactly?" he leaned forward in his chair, his wide eyes looking all the larger.

Again, Nuja hesitated. "For your own wellbeing." Katurian nodded slowly, "Is that the only reason?"

"Isn't that reason enough?"

Katurian smiled, that dab of blood from his lips smearing slightly over his crooked teeth. "Next question?"

Nuja sighed, sounding almost sympathetic. "I'm afraid there's no need. I'm not legally allowed to put you in harm's way, it goes against the entire purpose."

Katurian's soft eyes darkened in an instant. "No, Miss, I insist."

He did nothing actively threatening, but at the very least, Nuja no longer believed he was a pushover. He did not look eager to fight, per se, but she caught sight of a reservoir of power inside of this boy. It knocked her off her game. "Katurian, I could lose my job if I don't turn you away at this point."

His jaw twitched strangely, all nuances of which were visible in his starved face. "I want to save a life."

"Save yours."

His entire demeanor greyed. They stared at one another in complete disillusionment. At last, he stood, and Nuja sat up a bit straighter. She picked up his ID and reached out to return it to him. The barrel of a gun was positioned directly in front of her left eye. Katurian cocked the small pistol.

"I'm terribly sorry," his voice wavered, but his hand did not. "I really insist we go through with this, Miss."

*   *   *

She did not ask why this was so important. She did not cry for help. She was not going to argue or barter. She was going to get through this nightmare as briskly as possible. Her life was the goal, and so she was perfectly obedient, even if she trembled.

They got through health history questions without any problems. Midway through, Katurian put his gun back in his pocket, under the too-long shirt. He sat back in his chair, drawing his knees to his chest. He was a child, which terrified her to her core.

"Have you had homosexual intercourse?" Nuja queried softly. Katurian frowned. "Consenting or not?"

"It doesn't matter."

The boy flinched. "Seems like it should matter."

Nuja clicked her tongue indifferently, "I'll just say no. That one is left over from the AIDS scare anyway."

After completing a few more questions and lying about his weight, Nuja stopped. Adrenaline prevented exhaustion, but she was still perplexed into idleness.

"What's wrong?" Katurian asked.

She looked at him flatly and whispered, "Aside from my life being threatened?"

He bit his lip. "I'm really sorry about that. But you were gonna make me leave."

"I can't just start draining your blood out there. You're obviously ineligible. And I'm not sure how much is safe to take from you."

Katurian drummed his fingers on his knees anxiously. "Well, I can help you with the last one. You're going to take it all."

Nuja momentarily forgot how to breathe. "You're making me murder you?"

"But I don't want you to get in trouble or anything. Maybe you could bring the gurney back here, say I'm embarrassed but wanna donate? I'll write a note to let everyone know I'm okay with this, that I'm making you. Sign it and everything. Will that work?"

"You're making me murder you."

Katurian's smile was patient. "If you don't mind, Miss, I would appreciate it. I was going to just do it the old-fashioned way, with razorblades. Only that felt like a terrible waste."

"Katurian. . ." She didn't think to wonder why he wouldn't use the gun in his pocket.

"Can you imagine?" His words bounced. "All that blood just. . . wasted. I have enough iron and I'm not sick."

"You *are* sick," Ms. Nuja hissed.

Katurian pouted. "Not in a way that anyone else will catch."

"You need help," Nuja insisted with quiet, vicious urgency, "Just go home and talk to your parents—"

He looked sad, but not for himself, for Nuja. "I can't do that. You're kind of overestimating me, Miss. Nobody can stand to be near me, especially the people who had to have me." He offered his best smile. It was gorgeous despite everything. "Can we please just do this? It'll be over before you know it, promise."

"I'll take you," she promised, "to someone who can help you."

"*You're* going to help me."

They stared at one another. He reached a hand past his loose shirt and into his pocket. Her entire demeanor greyed. She would not let him point a gun at her again.

"Fine," she conceded. "I'll do it."

*   *   *

Just beyond her and Katurian's walled off corner of the room, everything ran smoothly. Two large, open, trusting entrances. Free gifts as one entered and as one exited. Not a hint of security. Not one camera in this massive room. All smiles and laughs and jokes out there. Nuja wanted to vomit.

Instead, she kicked up the locks on the wheels of a gurney and proceeded to push it back behind the fake wall. When she returned to the main, open area, another nurse approached her.

"What's going on?"

Nuja could only muster a head shake as she proceeded to transport the rest of her necessary materials.

Apparently, she reeked of trauma. The nurse grabbed her arm. "What is going on? Should I. . ." She faltered, trying to read Nuja's expression, "Do I need to call someone?"

Nuja nodded, simplicity lightening her slowly and then ferociously. She whispered, "911. Be subtle. He's armed." Nuja broke away from her grasp.

"What are you doing? Don't go back!"

"If I don't, he'll come out here." There was a certainty that was frightening and convincing in Nuja's smile. "Just trust me."

*   *   *

Nuja pushed back Katurian's sleeve and turned his forearm in her small hands, looking for the perfect vein. Instead, she found several bruises and scars. They decorated his skin like an abstract painting. She stared breathlessly.

Katurian apologized in his inflection, "My left arm is just as bad." He fidgeted uncomfortably, as if she was staring at his naked form. "Should I flex or something? Would that make it easier to find?"

"No, it's alright," Nuja assured him, her hands suddenly gentler, that breath rushing out of her all at once. "There's not much place for them to hide, after all."

After checking that he had no applicable allergies, she wiped his inner arm clean. As she prepared the needle, she habitually recited, "I'm sorry, this might leave a mark." Katurian laughed, which brought her back to the present. Caught somewhere between a sob and a chortle, she punctured him, and screwed the proper tubing together.

Katurian gulped, transfixed by the image of his blood coursing out of him. "Jeez, that's kinda scary looking."

Nuja pulled up a chair beside him. "It would have been scarier with a razorblade."

Katurian nodded distractedly, gaping at the artificial artery that extended out of him, pooling very cleanly and distantly from him.

The two sat in silence for a long time. The flow of blood began to slow, and before she could stop herself, she told him that opening and closing his fist would help speed up the process. Naturally, he obeyed, and within five minutes, he had given a pint.

"Guess my blood is dying to get out," he joked.

"Mmhm," Nuja responded humorlessly, clamping the tubing as she replaced this bag with a new one.

"A quarter of the way through, right? Something like that?"

"Yes, Mr. Napels."

Katurian did not take particularly well to being addressed so formally. He ravenously pumped his hand in and out of a fist.

"I'm awful sorry, Miss Fola Nuja."

She blinked. "What for?"

"I probably ruined your whole day."

Her eyes locked on him. Katurian sheepishly shrugged and leaned his head back. "Never been dizzy sitting down before. It's weird."

Her gaze was merciless. He silenced himself for good under its pressure. His pumping dragged, until his hand merely stayed unfurled.

The realization leaked into Nuja's consciousness like a steadily sinking lifeboat. Why would Katurian use razor blades if he had a working gun? Did he not have a working gun? What had he been threatening her with? Did he have no real ammunition with which to harm her after all? Had she been tricked?

Did he have no intention of hurting her all along?

It was too late. His eyelids drifted shut and his breathing slowed. Nuja jumped to her feet, clamping the tube, preventing any more blood from escaping.

By this point, cops arrived on the scene.

"No!" Nuja shrieked, standing in front of the battered, unconscious boy, "I changed my mind! I don't need you, I need an ambulance!" She scooped up the blood bags and placed them on top of Katurian. "Put it back! It's his, I'll explain it all later, *just put it back in his little body right now*!"

Interview with Grace Dillow

On Beginnings

I joined Butler's literary magazine, *Manuscripts*, my freshman year. I came to college without a major, but, honestly, it was pretty obvious from the start that I wanted to read books all day and talk about what I found so cool about them. So it was no surprise when *Manuscripts* stood out so much to me at the student organization fair. At first, I was just a reader for the magazine. Editing was limited to making sure there weren't any glaring mistakes. When I took the Literary Editing class with Professor Furuness, though, my view of editing changed and I discovered the intricacies it entailed. The class gave us the opportunity to see the editing process from beginning to end: from creating an aesthetic for our own literary magazine to picking stories and art pieces to go along with that vision, all the way through content edits and publication. I had so much fun in that class because the work didn't feel like work. It was creating our own zine, putting on paper the things that got us excited about art and literary works. (Mine happened to be centered around things dark and creepy). Literary Editing made me realize that the behind-the-scenes people could show creativity, too.

Going to a university without a solid idea of what you like to do is always scary, but that class helped me find a passion I didn't know I had. At the end of the semester, I knew *Manuscripts* needed more structure in the editing department and we needed to be more involved in the creation of our own magazine. Building an editing team from the ground up was a challenge I wasn't sure how to tackle, but once I was able to find some like-minded folks up to the task, it was easy.

On Process

My process is pretty simple. I read through a piece once to get a feel for the author's intent and style. With my second read, I make notes on the positives and the negatives I see. That could be "Hey! I really love this comparison," or "I think this could read better if you worded it like this." At this stage, I try to ease the author into the editing process. By letting them know what they're doing that works and giving concrete suggestions as to what could be done better, the relationship is more productive. After the author responds to these edits, I come back with more global editing suggestions, such as "I think you could do more with the ending by taking it in this direction," or "Have you considered working this section in earlier?" Here, I want to show the author the potential I see for the piece as a whole. I think the most important thing when interacting with an author is to be clear with your intentions so that you can get the best results in the most efficient way. Remember, you're making changes to someone's art; it's personal and everyone will react to it differently.

Advice for Emerging Editors

My biggest piece of advice would be to rank your suggestions. What I mean is that you should have an idea of each edit's importance. Think of each edit as "make or break," "I could compromise," or "This isn't that important, but I think it's a good suggestion." Then compare your ideas with the author's points of contention and determine how to move forward. The editing process is fluid and you need to be able to compromise, but you also need to be firm where you think it is most important. It's definitely a partnership, not a solo act.

What an Editor Should Avoid

The worst thing you can do is to not relate with your author. If you don't understand where they're coming from on a point or what led them to their idea, you won't be able to see where the piece has potential to move. You need to understand your author's limitations, as well as your own. Remember that you're working with another human being, not just written words.

To Consider

1 When you learned that this case study would feature an undergraduate editor, what did you expect? How did this case study match up with your expectations? Did anything surprise you?

2 Compare and contrast this case study with the other ones you have read. What patterns are you seeing? What is unique about this one?

3 "Remember that you're working with another human being, not just written words," says Dillow. In her editing approach, how does Dillow show that she remembers she is working with a human being?

4 What can you learn from this case study—either from the marked-up manuscript or the interview?

5 If you were editing this story, is there anything you might have done differently— either in terms of general approach or any individual marks or comments? (Your answer to this question might reveal a good deal about your own editing style and sensibility.)

Sarah Tam

Short Fiction (Student Example)

The format of this case study is different than the others. Earlier, we mentioned that editors will occasionally divide the editing process into stages: global editing first, and then line editing. Such is the case here. Accordingly, this case study will start with the original submission, followed by a letter addressing global edits, before showing the line-edited version.

The editor, Sarah Tam, took classes in editing and writing at Butler University while appearing in various theatre productions. She graduated in 2017 and is a simulation technician at IU Health as well as a freelance writer and editor. She is currently honing her editing skills and dabbling in short stories of her own.

Submitted Manuscript

The following story was submitted by Carissa Marquardt to *Manuscripts,* which published the final version.

"Putrid Pistols"

TRACKLIST
01: Butterfly Jars *(written by Stevie Lloyd)*
02: Rome Antics *(written by Stevie Lloyd, Rhett Burke)*
03: Blurry Bedtime Stories *(written by Stevie Lloyd, Rhett Burke)*
04: Taxicab to Brooklyn *(written by Stevie Lloyd)*
05: Tattoos I'll Never Get *(written by Stevie Lloyd)*

TRACK 03: Blurry Bedtime Stories

I was nine when I had lemon water before bed for some reason, and for a week straight I was plagued with this recurring nightmare that had nothing to do with lemons but everything to do with water.

And yeah, I was drowning, but it wasn't like I found myself abandoned in the middle of the sea, thrashing and sinking, life leeching out of me as if the angry waves needed it for themselves. Instead it was dark and I was outside, lying on a surface that was probably a road – it smelled like tar – while it rained and rained. Angry waves were substituted here with angry rain drops, and I'm telling you, they were pissed. I couldn't move, and they took the opportunity to fill me up; every orifice in my face, they liked those spots in particular. Soon I couldn't breathe.

I'd wake up drenched, but in my own sweat, not the rain. By that point my sister had heard me kicking around my sheets, thrashing a little, and she had crawled onto the edge of my bed.

"It's a dream again," she'd say. "Think of something nice."

Stella really sucked at giving advice. We were twins, and I remember being great at that, but *she* always said the same thing every time I woke like this that week. *Think of something nice, Stevie. Think of something nice.*

By the last few days of my nightmare plague, I'd fall asleep again to her little mantra like it was nice enough itself. I guess it was, at the time. When she got sick and died I wanted it engraved on her tombstone but our parents didn't understand it and they wouldn't listen to me because I was only nine.

Think of something nice, I remind myself nightly now. I don't have nightmares anymore (but I still avoid lemon water before bed). I don't really dream at all. Still, maybe my brain might conjure up something one of these nights if I could just *think of something nice*.

TRACK 01: Butterfly Jars

I knew I had to get out of Moorberry in high school. There was nothing wrong with the town, I just couldn't stand my parents any longer. I didn't even graduate, which I regret (kind of).

Mom wanted to leave Dad but she couldn't afford to, and Dad thought Mom was cheating on him even though she wasn't, and they had a *lot* of hospital bills piled up thanks to Stella. I don't blame her for our family falling apart, so I hope she doesn't blame me for leaving it as soon as I could afford my own vehicle.

I got a dog that I named Anya after a character from a movie Stella and I used to watch. To be honest I didn't think this decision through, but eventually I was glad I did it. I just didn't want to be alone once I left home, and I missed having a twin, and even though Anya can't be my new twin at least I could claim to not be talking to myself when I catch strangers' eyes a lane over at stoplights.

I don't think I intended to do music when I left originally, but it happened. I was in Madison, Wisconsin, on my way to Chicago, and I had time to kill before I continued on – wanted to avoid rush hour traffic. I don't remember what the music store was called anymore, but I went inside and recalled playing clarinet for my school's band. They had clarinets in all sorts of colors at that store. The rental I used to use at school was just black.

Before I got in trouble for bringing Anya inside with me, I saw this guitar that I liked a lot. I couldn't play it, but I decided I wanted to. I didn't buy it that day because I didn't have any money, but in Chicago I stayed with an older cousin for a while, got a job at some really trashy restaurant that didn't care about their employees having diplomas, sold my car, and *then* I bought a guitar.

My favorite place to practice was on the roof of my cousin's apartment building, which he had access to because he knew the right people. But he wasn't the only one, so by the time I started claiming that spot as my own, others had already left their marks. Someone drew bad chalk drawings on the ground. Someone strung up fairy lights around the doorway that weren't plugged in. Someone left two fold-up chairs and an umbrella in one corner, and someone left jars full of butterflies.

They were there the first time my cousin let me up there, and they were there every day after. Well, I mean, one day I noticed that one of the butterflies had died and then I knew that they all would eventually, so I released them. But while they were alive and well and the promise of death eluded them, I liked them a lot. At night especially, city lights reflected off them like little spotlights. A bokeh filter from a photo-editing app is what my every evening looked like.

The day after I set the butterflies free, all the empty jars that I'd left there had been smashed. I don't know if the person who owned them had done it or if another roof-goer was the culprit, but I felt like it was my fault, so I got a broom and cleaned up the mess. A week later I cut my foot on a shard of glass I must have missed, but I learned how to play that guitar.

TRACK 04: Taxicab to Brooklyn

I took Anya and my guitar to New York. Of course I did – that's where all aspiring musicians go. And we lived out of disgusting hotel rooms for three months before I finally met someone who was trying to do the same thing I was, and thank *god* she lived in an apartment.

Her name was Cleo and she played a keyboard that she called Salem. I never named my guitar. Cleo and I weren't similar enough in that way, and honestly we weren't very similar in any way other than wanting to make music, so that's about all we did together.

One night she left her phone at the apartment when she went out. She went out a lot, so that part wasn't weird, but what was weird was that it was three hours past the time she said she'd be home and she's never late. I don't know if we were friendly enough with each other to warrant my going out to look for her, but I did it anyway.

Anya didn't like the taxi very much. She rested her chin on my lap the entire time and whimpered occasionally, but it felt like any other taxi to me. It smelled a bit like weed, though. The driver didn't talk to me at all until I had to pay him.

I went to this club in Brooklyn she's mentioned in passing a few times and looked for hours before I figured she must not be there. Anya didn't like the club very much either, keeping her body pressed against my leg while I searched the place.

It was interesting though, I'll admit. I usually avoided the club scene because people in general weren't really my thing. Maybe I'd go if I had a group of friends to prevent strangers from trying to talk to me, but I didn't have a group of friends. I had Anya, and most of the people we passed were wearing things they didn't want anywhere near a dog, so I guess – like usual – she's the only friend I need.

We went back to the apartment and I never saw Cleo again. She didn't come back for any of her things – not even Salem – and I heard nothing in the news that might indicate something grim. She just. . .vanished. New York was weird.

I couldn't afford the apartment on my own, so I had to look for a roommate, which I didn't know how to do in a city where I knew no one. I put an ad in the paper, because that's how I first came across Anya.

TRACK 02: Rome Antics

My new roommate was a girl named Gemma who didn't play any instrument and had no interest in writing music with me. But she had a lot of friends and they all kind of adopted me, and the next thing I knew, a friend whose dad owned a little college coffee joint somewhere hooked me up with a gig. So I guess Gemma and her friends weren't that bad.

I didn't have enough material to play my own songs, but I could cover a Gabrielle Aplin track pretty well and figured I could probably just make the rest up as I went along.

This was a horrible idea. I was announced – "Stevie Lloyd, everybody," – and my gig lasted for two songs. I remembered that I could play "Flowers in the Window" by Travis because it wasn't very hard, and then no one had any requests I could actually play. Even Anya, sitting beside me, looked humiliated.

The guy who requested something by Fleetwood Mac caught me afterwards and asked if my name was really Stevie or if I was just copying Stevie Nicks. I hated him for that. He was probably a few years older than I was and needed a haircut, waves like defeated curls framing a sharp jawline and cheekbones that could cut glass. Anya stood on hind legs to put her front paws on his shoulders and nose at his chin, his neck, the collarbones slightly exposed beneath the loose white T-shirt he wore, before I could respond. Traitor.

I took Anya home, and then he took *me* home, but I didn't even get his name that night. The next morning over coffee I learned it was Rhett, which was a stupid name. I asked him if it was fake, if he was just copying it from *Gone with the Wind,* and I think he laughed but never actually answered the question.

Anya liked him a lot, which made spending time with him a common occurrence. He didn't do the singing thing, but he played guitar and taught me what he knew, which was far more than I did. We mostly practiced at his place. Gemma didn't like the noise. *Any* noise. I guess I stopped hating him at some point.

After a month of this, Gemma's friend got me a gig at the same college coffee joint, and it went a lot better. Rhett watched from his same table and requested the same Fleetwood Mac song, but this time I could play it. Anya sat herself beside my stool on the tiny stage the whole time. When I finished all five songs I had planned to play, I held a hand out in her direction, and she pawed at it in as close to a high five as she could manage.

Gigs like that one continued to follow, mostly thanks to Rhett, but also from being in the right place at the right time. Eventually I started making money from them instead of having to pay to get the gigs. And I ditched the covers for my own stuff. For the first time since Stella died twelve years ago, I told someone about that stupid recurring nightmare I'd had for a week from the lemon water. He helped me translate it into sheet music and lyrics.

One night when we were both really drunk, I let Rhett cut my hair. When we were sober we realized it didn't look too bad, so I dyed it black and gave my act a name. Anya and I became the Putrid Pistols thanks to inspiration from two of Rhett's tattoos, and people actually liked us. Rhett especially, it seemed.

TRACK 05: Tattoos I'll Never Get

Drinking became a problem for me eventually. I blamed Rhett so that I didn't have to blame myself, and then I continued to blame him for a lot of things that weren't his fault. Whatever we were doing together, I called it off after about a week of arguing. We were beginning to sound too much like my parents, and I got away from them for a reason.

Gemma helped me stop drinking. It took a few months, and I failed so often it felt like I'd never succeed, but then I did. And Gemma somehow knew I would. We didn't have much in common, but she was probably the best friend outside of Anya I'd ever had, which I hadn't seen coming when she moved in.

Later that year I turned twenty-two and I was still doing music, but I was doing different music. I don't know if I liked it any more than I liked the stuff I wrote with Rhett, but I felt like *I* was different from when I was with him, so my music should reflect that. I don't know if it did. I didn't have anyone to bounce ideas off of anymore. But I didn't have anyone to argue with either.

These new songs were just as successful. I started considering recording them. Would anyone buy an album of my lyrics? My thoughts, my feelings, my secrets, my ramblings, my babbling? It seemed unlikely. Seemed daunting. *Think of something nice.* Maybe I will. Maybe I won't.

I missed Rhett. Anya did too. Another night when we were drunk together, we came up with this ridiculous bucket list that was funny to read when we were sober. I had to tear it down from its place on my wall because it wasn't funny anymore, *especially* sober.

But a few of the things on that list weren't so weird, like visiting the deli from *When Harry Met Sally*'s fake orgasm scene. Maybe I could do that alone, or with Anya. She didn't like that film as much as Rhett did, but at least she didn't fight with me (even when I deserved it).

I was finally, truly sober, though. Maybe Rhett wouldn't fight with me anymore. I should call him. Maybe not. *Think of something nice. . .*

TRACK 06: Chardonnay Lipstick

There was a power outage in the city one evening. I took Anya to Central Park because I didn't want to stay indoors, and the weather was nice enough. Gemma actually accompanied us.

We weren't the only ones with the idea. Soon I found myself people-watching on a bench while Gemma played fetch with Anya. One woman in particular I remember because she looked like a fictional character straight out of a book I'd read in high school.

There was a lot to notice about her, but the most vivid were her lips, painted the color of

* * *

FOR ANYA

TRACKLIST

01: Putrid Pistol *(written by Rhett Burke)*

TRACK 01: Putrid Pistol (written by Rhett Burke)

The worst thing to happen to a writer is finding yourself unable to finish a piece of work for one reason or another. And that's what happened with Stevie and whatever song she had been working on when the college coffee joint where we met was held up at gunpoint. A lot of things happened in the nine minutes before the whole ordeal was over. Some of those things were stray bullets.

I couldn't find the notebook she was probably writing in. When I went to search for it, I started at the table I was sitting at when I watched her cover "Flowers in the Window" because that's where she would have sat. It wasn't on the floor and it wasn't on the table – it wasn't on *any* table or on the floor at all, anywhere. But she had been writing. Witnesses who recognized her had seen it.

Gemma gave me what few possessions Stevie had had, and I didn't really know what to do with all of it, so I found her family and sent most of it back to them. There was a keyboard called Salem that I kept, and her guitar. She never named that.

I guess I kept Anya too. And I guess I decided to try the singing thing finally, but only for her. She seemed to like it enough, although I can never seem to take away her blank puppy stare like she's given up looking at the world entirely since the one thing she wanted to see wasn't in it anymore.

If only dogs could talk. Anya was with Stevie like usual that day. She was the only dog I knew who could get into almost any establishment in this city. She was a Putrid Pistol, after all. Now the only one.

Global Edits

Dear Carissa,

I just finished rereading "Putrid Pistols – EP", and I was struck all over again by the honesty and straightforwardness of Stevie's narration, as well as the album form of the story. I'm excited to start working with you. Before we get into more in-depth line and paragraph edits, there are a few big-picture topics I'd like to go over.

One aspect that makes this story really special is how it's presented to the reader: in explanations of the tracks on Stevie's EP. Right now, the transitions between the tracks still read as a mostly continuous narrative, with the track titles interspersed in the appropriate places. What would happen if you tweaked the sections into more stand-alone pieces within the whole of the story? For example, the transition between the first and second sections jumps many years and topics, but it's still easy for the reader to understand what's happening. What if you tried this same sort of sudden change for the other transitions? I think it would amplify the effect that the form of the story has and make it even more impactful. I was also a little confused about when in the context of the story Stevie was writing these track descriptions. After some consideration, I decided that I thought she wrote them as she wrote the songs and reflected on whatever life event brought her to that particular song. I think that this journal-like aspect will be clearer if each of the sections were more distinguished from the others.

That being said, I think there are elements that can unify the sections more through theme than continuity of narrative. I love the idea of Stevie thinking back on her sister telling her to think of something nice. It seems to me that this gets at the heart of the story; that Stevie is always searching for that something nice. What do you think about highlighting that concept, if not that specific phrase, in the other sections (not just the first and last) to give an overall sense of unity to the story? I think this will help the story feel even more focused and purposeful.

One last aspect I'd like to address is the ending. I love that Rhett takes over the narrative, and I think that works really well for the story. I do also think that if you develop his character more throughout the sections he shows up in previously, his need to honor Stevie with his own music will make more sense to the audience. Maybe you could spend a little more time describing Stevie and Rhett's relationship before they break up? I think that this would raise the stakes of his tribute and allow that final section a greater sense of gravity.

Feel free to contact me with any questions or comments about any of these suggestions! Just to reiterate, this is your story and you have the final say on any and all edits. Do you think you could have a revised draft to me by this Friday, April 7? The next step would then be a round of line edits, which I would have to you by Monday, April 10. Thank you in advance for your work on this story!

Sincerely,

Sarah Tam

Revised Manuscript with Editing Marks

"Putrid Pistols"

TRACKLIST
01: Butterfly Jars *(written by Stevie Lloyd)*
02: Smitten *(written by Stevie Lloyd, Rhett Burke)*
03: Blurry Bedtime Stories *(written by Stevie Lloyd, Rhett Burke)*
04: Taxicab to Brooklyn *(written by Stevie Lloyd)*
05: Tattoos I'll Never Get *(written by Stevie Lloyd)*
06: Rome Antics *(written by Stevie Lloyd, Rhett Burke)*

TRACK 03: Blurry Bedtime Stories

I was nine when I had lemon water before bed, and for a week straight I was plagued with this recurring nightmare that had nothing to do with lemons but everything to do with water.

> Cutting this will simplify the sentence and make the reader's entrance to the piece smoother.

I was drowning, but it wasn't like I found myself abandoned in the middle of the sea, thrashing and sinking, life leeching out of me as if the angry waves needed it for themselves. Instead it was dark and I was outside, lying on a surface that was probably a road – it smelled like tar – while it rained and rained. Angry waves were substituted for angry rain drops, and I'm telling you, they were pissed. I couldn't move, and they took the opportunity to fill me up; ~~every hollow in my face,~~ they liked the hollows in my face~~those spots~~ in particular. Soon I couldn't breathe.

> Again, cutting any extra words will ease the reader into the piece.

> This will help streamline this sentence.

I'd wake up drenched, but in my own sweat, not the rain. By that point my sister had heard me kicking around my sheets, thrashing a little, and she had crawled onto the edge of my bed.

"It's a dream again," she'd say. "Think of something nice."

Stella really sucked at giving advice. We were twins, and I remember being great at advice, but *she* always said the same thing every time I woke from my nightmare that week. *Think of something nice, Stevie. Think of something nice.*

By the last few days of my nightmare plague, I'd fall asleep again to her little mantra like it was nice enough itself. I guess it was, at the time. When she got sick and died I wanted it engraved on her tombstone but our parents didn't understand it and they wouldn't listen to me because I was only nine.

> This sentence feels a little out of place here, maybe because of the reference of Stevie talking to herself – it seems to be dealing more with her feeling crazy than lonely.

Think of something nice, I remind myself nightly now. I don't have nightmares anymore (but I still avoid lemon water before bed). I don't really dream at all. Still, maybe my brain might conjure up a prettier image one of these nights if I could just *think of something nice.*

TRACK 01: v\\\ Jars

I knew I had to get out of Moorberry in high school. There was nothing wrong with the town, I just couldn't stand my parents any longer. I didn't even graduate, which I regret (kind of).

Shortly after leaving, I got a dog and named her Anya after a character from a movie Stella and I used to watch. To be honest I didn't think this decision through, but eventually I was glad I got her. I just didn't want to be alone, and I missed having a twin.

> In this section, you talk about two major topics – the guitar and Anya. You start with the guitar, then switch to talking about Anya, then switch back to the guitar. Is there a way you could separate the two out? Keep them in the same section still, but maybe talk about Anya first and then the guitar? Right now I feel like switching back and forth nullifies the importance each of them has to Stevie because they get in each other's way.

I didn't intend to do music when I left , but it happened. I was in Madison, Wisconsin, on my way to Chicago, and I had time to kill before <u>Anya and</u> I continued on – wanted to avoid rush hour traffic. I don't remember what the music store was called anymore, but I went inside, recalling playing clarinet for my school's band. They had clarinets in all sorts of colors at that store. The rental I used to use at school was just black.

> Now that you've moved the section about Anya to the beginning, can you add one detail here about where she is when Stevie goes in the music store?

> I think this helps clarify the sentence structure.

I saw this guitar that I liked a lot. I couldn't play it, but I decided I wanted to. I didn't buy it that day because I didn't have any money, but in Chicago I stayed with an older cousin for a while, got a job at some really trashy restaurant that didn't care about their employees having diplomas, sold my car, and *then* I bought a guitar.

My favorite place to practice was on the roof of my cousin's apartment building, which he had access to because he knew the right people. But he wasn't the only one, so by the time I started laying a claim to that spot, others had already left their marks. Someone drew bad chalk drawings on the ground. Someone strung up fairy lights around the doorway that weren't plugged in. Someone left two fold-up chairs and an umbrella in one corner, and someone left jars full of butterflies.

They were there the first time my cousin let me up there, and they were there every day after. Well, I mean, one day I noticed that one of the butterflies had died, and then I realized that they all would eventually, so I released them. But while they were alive and well and the promise of death eluded them, I liked them a lot. At night especially, city lights reflected off them like little spotlights.

> This reference feels pretty out of place, since none of the rest of story has any reference to distinctly modern technology.

The day after I set the butterflies free, all the empty jars that I'd left there had been smashed. I don't know if the person who owned them had done it or if another roof-goer was the culprit, but I felt like it was my fault, so I got a broom and cleaned up the mess. A week later I cut my foot on a shard of glass I must have missed, but I learned how to play that guitar.

TRACK 04: Taxicab to Brooklyn

When I moved to New York, my roommate's name was Cleo. Cleo and I weren't very similar in any way other than wanting to make music, so that's about all we did together. She played a keyboard that she called Salem. I never named my guitar. Our music was about the only thing we had in common.

> I like the work you did with the first round of revisions – I've just rearranged some things so that it flows a little more smoothly.

One night she left her phone at the apartment when she went out. She went out a lot, so that part wasn't weird; what was weird was that it was three hours past the time she said she'd be home and she's never late. I don't know if we were friendly enough with each other to warrant going out to look for her, but I did anyway.

> I think splitting this up into two sentences helps reinforce the strength of repeating the word weird.

Anya didn't like the taxi very much. She rested her chin on my lap the entire time and whimpered occasionally. Though she couldn't understand me, I found myself whispering, "Think of something nice," every so often to her.

> This takes the focus away from Anya and her reactions to the situation in this moment.

I went to this club in Brooklyn Cleo mentioned in passing a few times and looked for hours before I figured she must not be there. Anya didn't like the club very much either. She kept her body pressed against my leg while I searched the place.

> I really love this tie-in to the first section! Nice work!

We went back to the apartment and I never saw Cleo again. She didn't come back for any of her things – not even Salem – and I heard nothing in the news that might indicate something grim. She just. . .vanished. New York was weird.

> I would use Cleo's name here to remind the audience who they're looking for.

I couldn't afford the apartment on my own, so I had to look for a roommate, which I didn't know how to do in a city where I knew no one. I put an ad in the paper, because that's how I first came across Anya. It took three days before I received a response.

> The ending of this section seems a little abrupt. Could you add even one more sentence, maybe about waiting to hear from a potential roommate or even another tie-in to "think of something nice", just to strengthen the resolution here?

> This is good! It's a nice tie-in to the beginning of the next section.

TRACK 02: Smitten

My new roommate was a girl named Gemma who didn't play any instrument and had no interest in writing music with me. But she had a lot of friends and I guess they weren't that bad. They all kind of adopted me, and the next thing I knew, a friend whose dad owned a little college coffee joint somewhere hooked me up with a gig.

This was a horrible idea. I was announced – "Stevie Lloyd, everybody," – and my gig lasted for two songs. I didn't have enough material to play my own music, but I could cover a Gabrielle Aplin track pretty well and figured I could just make up the rest as I went along. I remembered I could do "Flowers in the Window" by Travis because it wasn't very hard, but then no one had any requests I could actually play. Even Anya, sitting beside me, looked humiliated.

A ~~The~~ guy who requested something by Fleetwood Mac caught me afterwards and asked if my name was really Stevie or if I was just copying Stevie Nicks. I hated him for that. He was probably a few years older than I was and needed a haircut, waves like defeated curls framing a sharp jawline and cheekbones that could cut glass. Anya stood on hind legs to put her front paws on his shoulders and nose at his chin, his neck, his collarbones, before I could respond. Traitor.

> This change makes all three items in the list uniform. There were also a lot of details about Rhett's appearance in this section and it was a little overwhelming. I really like the line about the curls and cheekbones, so I cut the comment about his t-shirt. What do you think?

I took Anya home, and then he took *me* home, but I didn't even get his name that night. The next morning over coffee I learned it was Rhett, which was a stupid name. I asked him if his name was really Rhett or ~~it was fake,~~ if he was just copying it from *Gone with the Wind,* and I think he laughed but never actually answered the question.

> If you word this the same as Rhett's earlier comment, it's easier for the reader to make the connection and get the joke.

Anya liked him a lot, which made spending time with him a common occurrence. He didn't do the singing thing, but he played guitar and taught me what he knew, which was far more than I did. We mostly practiced at his place. Gemma didn't like the noise. I guess I stopped hating him at some point.

> This makes Gemma seem a little too mean and picky, especially since she and Stevie are friends later.

After a month of Rhett and I practicing and learning how to share our days with each other, Gemma's friend got me another gig at the same coffee joint, and it went a lot better. Rhett watched from his same table and requested the same Fleetwood Mac song, but this time I could play it. Anya sat ~~herself~~ beside my stool on the tiny stage the whole time. When I finished all five songs I had planned to play, I held a hand out in her direction, and she pawed at it in as close to a high five as she could manage.

> I'd leave this out to highlight how good Rhett was for Stevie and his positive influence on her life.

Gigs like that one continued to follow, mostly thanks to Rhett. Eventually I started making money ~~from them~~ instead of having to pay to get the gigs. And I ditched the covers for my own stuff. For the first time since Stella died twelve years ago, I told someone about that stupid recurring nightmare I'd had for a week from the lemon water. Rhett helped me translate it into sheet music and lyrics.

> Who "them" referred to confused me briefly, so I think it makes more sense to cut these two words.

One night when we were both really drunk, I let him cut my hair. When we were sober we realized it didn't look too bad, so I dyed it black and gave my act a name. Anya and I became the Putrid Pistols, and people actually liked us. Rhett especially, it seemed.

TRACK 06: Rome Antics

We did a lot of things well together, Rhett and I, and my favorite of those things was fitting each other into our separate lives. It's not like we moved in together or anything, but we came as close as it gets to that before it's the real deal.

Mostly, what kept me from making the official move was the fact that Anya wasn't technically allowed inside his building. We had to sneak her in, and it only worked because she was well-behaved enough not to bark.

But a lot of my stuff wound up finding homes in his apartment, and it all seemed to look better there than it did at the place I shared with Gemma. Besides, she probably was grateful for all the extra space whenever Anya and I were gone. She recently got into *Buffy the Vampire Slayer*, and nobody gets between Gemma and Netflix and lives to tell the tale.

So I shared a bed with Rhett and Anya shared a bed with the sofa cushions, and it felt like this was how New York was always supposed to feel: small. . .home. Perhaps this was something nice.

Another thing we did well together was dating. To be fair, the city made it easy to be good at it. Every Friday after a gig we'd try different bars, one a night until we found the best one in a particular area. The last Saturday of every month found us at Black Tap for the best milkshakes New York had to offer. Tuesday mornings were for Anya, spent walking to different dog parks and getting breakfast at dog-friendly cafés.

On a particularly cool Friday evening after we left the wedding reception we'd crashed for the free bar, Rhett tucked me away beneath his jacket and we found ourselves walking the High Line at three in the morning.

There was a little bundle of flowers growing in the center of two crossing train tracks. Though the city offered more light than one would expect in the dead of the night – at least in the Meatpacking District – it was next to impossible to identify what kind of flowers they were until Rhett stepped off the path and plucked one for me, no one around to witness his rule-breaking but me. Daisies.

When we returned to his apartment, Anya was happy to cuddle us both until our bones stopped chattering from the cold. I taped the daisy to his wall, right above the strip of photobooth pictures we'd taken with Anya.

TRACK 05: Tattoos I'll Never Get

Drinking became a problem for me. I blamed Rhett so that I didn't have to blame myself, and then I continued to blame him for a lot of things that weren't his fault. I called it off after about a week straight of arguing. We were beginning to sound too much like my parents, and I got away from them for a reason.

Gemma helped me stop drinking. I'll never forget the look on her face when I had to ask her for help. We didn't have much in common, but she was probably the best friend outside of Anya I'd ever had. It took a few months, and I failed so often it felt like I'd never succeed, but then I did. And Gemma somehow knew I would.

Margin comments:

This comment feels a little too catty for Stevie. I like the idea of using this space to reveal another detail about Gemma, but I think it might be better to say something about why she likes quiet (something about her job or personality) rather than having Stevie comment on her relationship.

How is NY supposed to feel? I think this is an interesting idea and I'm really curious about it. Could you add a colon and one phrase that describes this feeling more specifically?

This feels a little unnecessarily braggy. I love the specific details about what Stevie and Rhett did together, so I'd jump straight into those.

I love this section! This is exactly what the story needs to cement Stevie and Rhett's relationship to support the end. Nice work!

Since you added that last section, this comment doesn't quite work anymore. What about something like, "Even though we were basically living together, I called it off. . ."?

I'm curious about what a specific comment about how Gemma got pulled into Stevie's drinking problem would feel like here. Maybe she found Stevie passed out and then started helping? Or Stevie finally asked her for help? I think a specific comment would reinforce the progress Stevie makes and how good it is when she overcomes her drinking and moves on.

Later that year I turned twenty-two and I was still doing music, but I was doing different music. I don't know if I liked it any more than I liked the stuff I wrote with Rhett, but I felt like *I* was different from when I was with him. I wanted my music to reflect that. I don't know if it did. I didn't have anyone to bounce ideas off of anymore. But I didn't have anyone to argue with either.

> I got a little lost in this sentence, so I split it into two to makes it easier on the reader to follow.

These new songs were just as successful. I started considering recording them. Would anyone buy an album of my lyrics? My thoughts, my feelings, my secrets, my ramblings, my babbling? It seemed unlikely. Daunting. *Think of something nice.* Maybe I will. Maybe I won't.

> I think this makes the adjectives a little punchier, which will highlight the conflict Stevie is going through with her music and whether or not to record it.\\\

I missed Rhett. Anya did too. One night when we were drunk together, we came up with this ridiculous bucket list that was funny to read when we were sober. I had to tear it down from its place on my wall because it wasn't funny anymore, *especially* sober.

But a few of the things on that list weren't so weird, like visiting the deli from *When Harry Met Sally*'s fake orgasm scene. Maybe I could do that with Anya. She didn't like that film as much as Rhett did, but at least she didn't fight with me (even when I deserved it).

> I like how this reflects the section above about her uncertainty about her music!

I was finally, truly sober, though. Maybe Rhett wouldn't fight with me anymore. Maybe I should call him. Maybe not. Think of something nice . . .

TRACK 06: Chardonnay Lipstick

There was a power outage in the city last week. I took Anya to Central Park because I didn't want to stay indoors, and the weather was nice enough. Gemma actually accompanied us.

> An indicator of this episode happening previously might be all it takes to clear up the confusion around when and where the shooting happened.

We weren't the only ones with the idea. Soon I found myself people-watching on a bench while Gemma played fetch with Anya. One woman in particular I remember because she looked like a fictional character straight out of a book I'd read in high school.

There was a lot to notice about her, but most vivid were her lips, painted the color of

> Later, Rhett talks about Stevie being shot in a coffee shop. The way I read these two sections, this is the section that Stevie was writing when she got shot. Do you want to change this to coffee shop? Or change the later one to Central Park?

*   *   *

FOR ANYA
TRACKLIST
01: Putrid Pistol *(written by Rhett Burke)*

TRACK 01: Putrid Pistol (written by Rhett Burke)

The worst thing to happen to a writer is finding yourself unable to finish a piece of work for one reason or another. And that's what happened with Stevie and whatever song she had been working on when the college coffee joint

> If this is when Stevie gets shot, how does Gemma play into it? I guess I'm just a little confused about how Track 6 is related to Stevie's death. Are they the same incident?

> I'd like to have an entire blank page in between the end of track 6 and For Anya. I think it'll really build the suspense about what happened. Is that cool with you?

> I'd recommend changing this to something like "where she was" so that the audience doesn't get distracted from what's happening right now in the story.

...where we met and where she had been was held up at gunpoint. A lot of things happened in the nine minutes before the whole ordeal was over. Some of those things were stray bullets.

I couldn't find the notebook she was probably writing in. When I went to search for it, I started at the table I was sitting at when I watched her cover "Flowers in the Window" because that's where she always~~would have~~ sat. It wasn't on the floor and it wasn't on the table – it wasn't on *any* table or on the floor at all, anywhere. But she had been writing. Witnesses who recognized her had seen it.

Stevie had family, but they must not have kept in touch. Gemma gave me what few possessions Stevie had had, and I didn't really know what to do with all of it, so I found her family and sent most of it back to them. There was a keyboard called Salem that I kept, and her guitar. She never named that.

> Good! I like this. I think it strengthens the ending and makes is that much more powerful.

I kept Anya too. And I guess I decided to try the singing thing finally, but only for her. She seemed to like it enough, although I can never seem to take away her blank puppy stare. She looks like she's given up looking at the world entirely since the one thing she was looking for wasn't in it anymore.

> If only dogs could talk, then what? I think the story needs a little stronger of a resolution. Would Rhett record her songs if he could find her notebook? Would he publish her music? Also, one last tie-in of the "think of something nice" would be great if you could work it in here.

Once when Anya had a bad experience with a goose in Central Park, I heard Stevie tell her to *"think of something nice."* I wonder if Stevie managed to accomplish that herself. Perhaps her notebook. . . If only dogs could talk. Anya was with Stevie like usual that day. She was the only dog I knew who could get into almost any establishment in this city. She was a Putrid Pistol, after all. Now the only one.

Final Version

"Putrid Pistols"

TRACKLIST
01: Butterfly Jars *(written by Stevie Lloyd)*
02: Smitten *(written by Stevie Lloyd, Rhett Burke)*
03: Blurry Bedtime Stories *(written by Stevie Lloyd, Rhett Burke)*
04: Taxicab to Brooklyn *(written by Stevie Lloyd)*
05: Tattoos I'll Never Get *(written by Stevie Lloyd)*
06: Rome Antics *(written by Stevie Lloyd, Rhett Burke)*
07: Chardonnay Lipstick *(written by Stevie Lloyd)*

TRACK 03: Blurry Bedtime Stories

I was nine when I had lemon water before bed, and for a week straight I was plagued with this recurring nightmare that had nothing to do with lemons but everything to do with water.

I was drowning, but it wasn't like I found myself abandoned in the middle of the sea, thrashing and sinking, life leeching out of me as if the angry waves needed it for themselves. Instead it was dark and I was outside, lying on a surface that was probably a road – it smelled like tar – while it rained and rained. Angry waves were substituted for angry rain drops, and I'm telling you, they were pissed. I couldn't move, and they took the opportunity to fill me up; they liked the hollows in my face in particular. Soon I couldn't breathe.

I'd wake up drenched, but in my own sweat, not the rain. By that point my sister had heard me kicking around my sheets, thrashing a little, and she had crawled onto the edge of my bed.

"It's a dream again," she'd say. "Think of something nice."

Stella really sucked at giving advice. We were twins, and I remember being great at advice, but *she* always said the same thing every time I woke from my nightmare that week. *Think of something nice, Stevie. Think of something nice.*

By the last few days of my nightmare plague, I'd fall asleep again to her little mantra like it was nice enough itself. I guess it was, at the time. When she got sick and died I wanted it engraved on her tombstone but our parents didn't understand it and they wouldn't listen to me because I was only nine.

Think of something nice, I remind myself nightly now. I don't have nightmares anymore (but I still avoid lemon water before bed). I don't really dream at all. Still, maybe my brain might conjure up a prettier image one of these nights if I could just *think of something nice.*

TRACK 01: Butterfly Jars

I knew I had to get out of Moorberry in high school. There was nothing wrong with the town, I just couldn't stand my parents any longer. I didn't even graduate, which I regret (kind of).

Shortly after leaving, I got a dog and named her Anya after a character from a movie Stella and I used to watch. To be honest I didn't think this decision through, but eventually I was glad I got her. I just didn't want to be alone, and I missed having a twin.

I didn't intend to do music when I left, but it happened. I was in Madison, Wisconsin, on my way to Chicago, and I had time to kill before Anya and I continued on – wanted to avoid rush hour traffic. I don't remember what the music store was called anymore, but I went inside, recalling playing clarinet for my school's band. They had clarinets in all sorts of colors at that store. The rental I used to use at school was just black.

Before anyone noticed I'd brought a dog inside, I saw this guitar that I liked a lot. I couldn't play it, but I decided I wanted to. I didn't buy it that day because I didn't have any money, but in Chicago I stayed with an older cousin for a while, got a job at some really trashy restaurant that didn't care about their employees having diplomas, sold my car, and *then* I bought a guitar.

My favorite place to practice was on the roof of my cousin's apartment building, which he had access to because he knew the right people. But he wasn't the only one, so by the time I started laying a claim to that spot, others had already left their marks. Someone drew bad chalk drawings on the ground. Someone strung up fairy lights around the doorway that weren't plugged in. Someone left two fold-up chairs and an umbrella in one corner, and someone left jars full of butterflies.

They were there the first time my cousin let me up there, and they were there every day after. Well, I mean, one day I noticed that one of the butterflies had died, and then I realized that they all would eventually, so I released them. But while they were alive and well and the promise of death eluded them, I liked them a lot. At night especially, city lights reflected off them like little spotlights.

The day after I set the butterflies free, all the empty jars that I'd left there had been smashed. I don't know if the person who owned them had done it or if another roof-goer was the culprit, but I felt like it was my fault, so I got a broom and cleaned up the mess. A week later I cut my foot on a shard of glass I must have missed, but I learned how to play that guitar.

TRACK 04: Taxicab to Brooklyn

When I moved to New York, my roommate's name was Cleo. Cleo and I weren't very similar in any way other than wanting to make music, so that's about all we did together. She played a keyboard that she called Salem. I never named my guitar. Our music was about the only thing we had in common.

One night she left her phone at the apartment when she went out. She went out a lot, so that part wasn't weird; what was weird was that it was three hours past the time she said she'd be home and she's never late. I don't know if we were friendly enough with each other to warrant going out to look for her, but I did anyway.

Anya didn't like the taxi very much. She rested her chin on my lap the entire time and whimpered occasionally. Though she couldn't understand me, I found myself whispering, *"Think of something nice,"* every so often to her.

I went to this club in Brooklyn Cleo mentioned in passing a few times and looked for hours before I figured she must not be there. Anya didn't like the club very much either. She kept her body pressed against my leg while I searched the place.

We went back to the apartment and I never saw Cleo again. She didn't come back for any of her things – not even Salem – and I heard nothing in the news that might indicate something grim. She just. . .vanished. New York was weird.

I couldn't afford the apartment on my own, so I had to look for a roommate, which I didn't know how to do in a city where I knew no one. I put an ad in the paper, because that's how I first came across Anya. It took three days before I received a response.

TRACK 02: Smitten

My new roommate was a girl named Gemma who didn't play any instrument and had no interest in writing music with me. But she had a lot of friends and I guess they weren't that bad. They all kind of adopted me, and the next thing I knew, a friend whose dad owned a little college coffee joint somewhere hooked me up with a gig.

This was a horrible idea. I was announced – "Stevie Lloyd, everybody," – and my gig lasted for two songs. I didn't have enough material to play my own music, but I could cover a Gabrielle Aplin track pretty well and figured I could just make up the rest as I went along. I remembered I could do "Flowers in the Window" by Travis because it wasn't very hard, but then no one had any requests I could actually play. Even Anya, sitting beside me, looked humiliated.

A guy who requested something by Fleetwood Mac caught me afterwards and asked if my name was really Stevie or if I was just copying Stevie Nicks. I hated him for that. He was probably a few years older than I was and needed a haircut, waves like defeated curls framing a sharp jawline and cheekbones that could cut glass. Anya stood on hind legs to put her front paws on his shoulders and nose at his chin, his neck, his collarbones, before I could respond. Traitor.

I took Anya home, and then he took *me* home, but I didn't even get his name that night. The next morning over coffee I learned it was Rhett, which was a stupid name. I asked him if his name was really Rhett or if he was just copying it from *Gone with the Wind,* and I think he laughed but never actually answered the question.

Anya liked him a lot, which made spending time with him a common occurrence. He didn't do the singing thing, but he played guitar and taught me what he knew, which was far more than I did. We mostly practiced at his place. Gemma didn't like the noise. I guess I stopped hating him at some point.

After a month of Rhett and I practicing and learning how to share our days with each other, Gemma's friend got me another gig at the same coffee joint, and it went a lot better. Rhett watched from his same table and requested the same Fleetwood Mac song, but this time I could play it. Anya sat beside my stool on the tiny stage the whole time. When I finished all five songs I had planned to play, I held a hand out in her direction, and she pawed at it in as close to a high five as she could manage.

Gigs like that one continued to follow, mostly thanks to Rhett. Eventually I started making money instead of having to pay to get the gigs. And I ditched the covers for my own stuff. For the first time since Stella died twelve years ago, I told someone about that stupid recurring nightmare I'd had for a week from the lemon water. Rhett helped me translate it into sheet music and lyrics.

One night when we were both really drunk, I let him cut my hair. When we were sober we realized it didn't look too bad, so I dyed it black and gave my act a name. Anya and I became the Putrid Pistols, and people actually liked us. Rhett especially, it seemed.

TRACK 06: Rome Antics

We did a lot of things well together, Rhett and I, and my favorite of those things was fitting each other into our separate lives. It's not like we moved in together or anything, but we came as close as it gets to that before it's the real deal.

Mostly, what kept me from making the official move was the fact that Anya wasn't technically allowed inside his building. We had to sneak her in, and it only worked because she was well-behaved enough not to bark.

But a lot of my stuff wound up finding homes in his apartment, and it all seemed to look better there than it did at the place I shared with Gemma. Besides, she probably was grateful for all the extra space whenever Anya and I were gone. She recently got into *Buffy the Vampire Slayer,* and nobody gets between Gemma and Netflix and lives to tell the tale.

So I shared a bed with Rhett and Anya shared a bed with the sofa cushions, and it felt like this was how New York was always supposed to feel: small. . .home. Perhaps this was something nice.

Another thing we did well together was dating. To be fair, the city made it easy to be good at it. Every Friday after a gig we'd try different bars, one a night until we found the best one in a particular area. The last Saturday of every month found us at Black Tap for the best milkshakes New York had to offer. Tuesday mornings were for Anya, spent walking to different dog parks and getting breakfast at dog-friendly cafés.

On a particularly cool Friday evening after we left the wedding reception we'd crashed for the free bar, Rhett tucked me away beneath his jacket and we found ourselves walking the High Line at three in the morning.

There was a little bundle of flowers growing in the center of two crossing train tracks. Though the city offered more light than one would expect in the dead of the night – at least in the Meatpacking District – it was next to impossible to identify what kind of flowers they were until Rhett stepped off the path and plucked one for me, no one around to witness his rule-breaking but me. Daisies.

When we returned to his apartment, Anya was happy to cuddle us both until our bones stopped chattering from the cold. I taped the daisy to his wall, right above the strip of photobooth pictures we'd taken with Anya.

TRACK 05: Tattoos I'll Never Get

Drinking became a problem for me. I blamed Rhett so that I didn't have to blame myself, and then I continued to blame him for a lot of things that weren't his fault. I called it off after about a week straight of arguing. We were beginning to sound too much like my parents, and I got away from them for a reason.

Gemma helped me stop drinking. I'll never forget the look on her face when I had to ask her for help. We didn't have much in common, but she was probably the best friend outside of Anya I'd ever had. It took a few months, and I failed so often it felt like I'd never succeed, but then I did. And Gemma somehow knew I would.

Later that year I turned twenty-two and I was still doing music, but I was doing different music. I don't know if I liked it any more than I liked the stuff I wrote with Rhett, but I felt like *I* was different from when I was with him. I wanted my music to reflect that. I don't know if it did. I didn't have anyone to bounce ideas off of anymore. But I didn't have anyone to argue with either.

These new songs were just as successful. I started considering recording them. Would anyone buy an album of my lyrics? My thoughts, my feelings, my secrets, my ramblings, my babbling? It seemed unlikely. Daunting. *Think of something nice.*

Maybe I will. Maybe I won't.

I missed Rhett. Anya did too. One night when we were drunk together, we came up with this ridiculous bucket list that was funny to read when we were sober. I had to tear it down from its place on my wall because it wasn't funny anymore, *especially* sober.

But a few of the things on that list weren't so weird, like visiting the deli from *When Harry Met Sally*'s fake orgasm scene. Maybe I could do that with Anya. She didn't like that film as much as Rhett did, but at least she didn't fight with me (even when I deserved it).

I was finally, truly sober, though. Maybe Rhett wouldn't fight with me anymore. Maybe I should call him. Maybe not. *Think of something nice. . .*

TRACK 06: Chardonnay Lipstick

There was a power outage in the city last week. I took Anya to Central Park because I didn't want to stay indoors, and the weather was nice enough. Gemma actually accompanied us.

We weren't the only ones with the idea. Soon I found myself people-watching on a bench while Gemma played fetch with Anya. One woman in particular I remember because she looked like a fictional character straight out of a book I'd read in high school.

There was a lot to notice about her, but most vivid were her lips, painted the color of

FOR ANYA
TRACKLIST
01: Putrid Pistol *(written by Rhett Burke)*

TRACK 01: Putrid Pistol (written by Rhett Burke)

The worst thing to happen to a writer is finding yourself unable to finish a piece of work for one reason or another. And that's what happened with Stevie and whatever song she had been working on when the college coffee joint where we met and where she had been was held up at gunpoint. A lot of things happened in the nine minutes before the whole ordeal was over. Some of those things were stray bullets.

I couldn't find the notebook she was probably writing in. When I went to search for it, I started at the table I was sitting at when I watched her cover "Flowers in the Window" because that's where she always sat. It wasn't on the floor and it wasn't on the table – it wasn't on *any* table or on the floor at all, anywhere. But she had been writing. Witnesses who recognized her had seen it.

Stevie had family, but they must not have kept in touch. Gemma gave me what few possessions Stevie had had, and I didn't really know what to do with all of it, so I found her family and sent most of it back to them. There was a keyboard called Salem that I kept, and her guitar. She never named that.

I kept Anya too. And I guess I decided to try the singing thing finally, but only for her. She seemed to like it enough, although I can never seem to take away her blank puppy stare. She looks like she's given up looking at the world entirely since the one thing she was looking for wasn't in it anymore.

Once when Anya had a bad experience with a goose in Central Park, I heard Stevie tell her to *"think of something nice."* I wonder if Stevie managed to accomplish that herself. Perhaps her notebook. . . If only dogs could talk. Anya was with Stevie like usual that day. She was the only dog I knew who could get into almost any establishment in this city. She was a Putrid Pistol, after all. Now the only one.

Interview with Sarah Tam

On Beginning

I've been editing for so long that I can't remember when I started, but until recently I stuck to editing my own and my classmates' work. At first I edited out of necessity, for school assignments. But after years of peer editing in class and being upset when my own papers came back with hardly any comments, I realized that I really enjoyed picking apart a piece of writing and trying to make it better.

In my sophomore year of college, a friend asked me to edit their paper for a class. I warned them that I'd rip it apart (probably not the best phrasing, but I wanted them to know what they were getting into!). I proceeded to cover the entire paper in green ink, filling the margins with corrections, comments, and questions. Ever since then, I've been hooked.

On Process

This is something I'm still figuring out for myself! After trying many different styles, I've found that I really like to have the manuscript printed out and physically in front of me. I want to be able to write all over in the margins and make markings on the lines themselves (and sometimes draw pictures just for fun!). I think having the text printed helps me to focus on it. If I am editing something on a computer, though, I like to read it through and write down on a separate paper places that strike me as needing work. That way I don't have to figure out how to fix it right away and I'm able to get a better overall understanding of the manuscript. Then I'll go back through and figure out how to edit the spots that stuck out to me. I'll frequently read it through as many times as I can, because I'll almost always catch things I missed on the first several reads.

Keys to Being a Good Editor

I think the most important thing is to build an open, honest channel of communication with the writer. They have to know that they're allowed to agree or disagree with you, and that your feedback is intended to improve their work, not discourage them. I look at editing as helping the writer make the work the best version of itself, so a willingness to meet the work on its own terms is also key. Also, there's no substitute for having good attention to detail and an ability to focus on different levels. You want to be able to edit on the sentence level, the paragraph level, and the overall work. That way, you can make sure that every part of the writer's work is part of a comprehensive whole.

On What an Editor Should Avoid

I think one of the traps that editors fall into is imposing their own writing style or preferences onto the manuscript. There's a difference between not liking something and that thing not being good. Now, I think the editing process goes better in general if the editor likes the manuscript, but still, the editor has to be careful to preserve the author's voice and style, rather than forcing the work into something it doesn't want to be.

Why She Edits

One of the things I enjoy most about editing is feeling like I'm on a treasure hunt. I like to search for the best parts of the story and excavate them from the maybe not-as-good parts surrounding them. There's something satisfying about helping a story take shape and become better than it was before you worked on it. I also love the nitty-gritty, line to line details. I enjoy making sentences flow and making sure that all of the commas are in the right place; it appeals to the hyper-organized side of my brain.

To Consider

1 Here's an argument: *Editing is about paying attention in a deep and sustained way. Editing is the art of giving a shit about a manuscript—about <u>everything</u> in that manuscript, no matter how small.*

Here's another argument: Tam's approach is the embodiment of that philosophy. What is your response to that philosophy and Tam's approach?

2 "One of the things I enjoy most about editing is feeling like I'm on a treasure hunt," says Tam. Finish this line for yourself: *One of the things I enjoy most about editing is* _____.

3 By this point in the book, you're probably getting a good sense of your own traits and tendencies. As an editor, how are you similar to Tam? How are you different? Describe yourself as the editor you are right now, not the editor you aspire to be.

4 Describe yourself as the editor you aspire to be.

Test Editing
From Observation
to Practice

If the last section was the surgery theater, this section is where we hand you a scalpel. We'll walk you through different editing strategies and techniques, following each guided exercise with reflection questions so you can process what you're learning.

To encourage the type of risk-taking necessary for learning, we'll keep the stakes low on these exercises by encouraging you to practice your moves on one of the CPR Dummy stories included in the appendix. Do what you want to the Dummy; the author won't complain. If you would rather practice with a "live manuscript," though, we won't stop you.

The exercises in this section are designed to be practiced in the order in which they appear, proceeding from the big moves of global editing to the tightening and polishing of line-editing. The movement is from whole to parts, higher order operations to lower order operations.

We created this progression, broken down into stages, for the purpose of learning, not as a reflection of how experienced editors operate in the wild. Yes, sometimes experienced editors *do* break the process into stages. As noted earlier in the book, editors will occasionally handle global editing as its own step before moving on to line editing, especially if the manuscript needs structural changes. But if the manuscript is structurally sound, the experienced editor may handle both types of editing at once, moving freely between multiple levels and editing operations.

> You will learn more about levels and operations in the first exercise in this section.

In this way, the editing process often resembles the writing process as recursive and non-linear. Typically, a writer does not complete one discrete stage at a time: first planning, and then pre-writing, and then composing, before finally revising. Most writers will move between these stages, sometimes in the course of crafting a single line. So it is with editing: an experienced editor may flit between levels during a single editing pass.

We hope that you can work in this non-linear way, too—eventually. First, let's get to know some techniques, one by one. Call this the Miyagi approach: Learn one move at a time and put it all together later.

Global Editing

Goal: To learn how to focus on big-picture suggestions about a manuscript, and how to communicate those suggestions to a writer.

> The ideas in this essay owe a great deal to "Revision Strategies of Student Writers and Experienced Adult Writers" by Nancy Sommers.

Novice editors are dachshunds. Experienced editors are hawks.

Let us explain.

Typically, novice editors are good at working on the line-level of a manuscript, tightening and polishing sentences. Mainly this involves little snips and substitutions. Rewording. Clarifying. Like dachshunds, they sniff along the sentences, seeing each part clearly, but unable to get a view of the whole.

A hawk, on the other hand, can soar high enough to see the whole hunting ground—and it can dive down to the grass before flapping back up again. So it is with experienced editors, who can see the big picture, but can also zoom in to a line, a phrase, a word.

Like novices, experienced editors snip and substitute, but sometimes they make bigger cuts. Or point to places where material might be added. Or suggest a different sequence. As they edit parts, they keep in mind how their suggested changes would affect the whole.

Novice editors may see the potential in a line, but experienced editors see the opportunities and potential in a manuscript.

Novice Editors	Experienced Editors
See individual parts	See the whole
Operate on three levels: • Word • Phrase • Sentence	Operate on five levels: • Word • Phrase • Sentence • Overall structure/architecture • Meaning
Perform three operations: • Substitution • Deletion • Asking for clarification	Perform seven operations: • Substitution • Deletion • Asking for clarification • Addition • Reordering/Resequencing • Asking bigger questions • Pointing to opportunities

Which brings us to the big question: How does an editor migrate from the left column to the right column?

Answer: By learning how to edit globally.

Ready to learn by doing? Start with a manuscript (which can be a CPR Dummy Story found in the appendix, or a piece that your teacher provides) and follow the steps below.

Practice

To Do

Step 1: To get a holistic view of the manuscript, read the whole thing without making any marks on the page.

At this point, you will be visited by a devil. He will tell you it's okay to make a few changes as you read. In fact, you'd better make those changes, or you'll forget them later.

That devil is not your friend. The instant you jot a note on the page, you'll have zoomed in to the line level, which will make it hard to get a hawk's-eye view of the whole manuscript.

Here's a zen koan of editing: The first step is not-editing.

Step 2: Read the manuscript again. As you read, think about the architecture of the manuscript, the components and their sequence, how they relate to one another. Think about character and meaning, and what this story is trying to become so you can honor that trajectory.

At this point you will be visited by another devil. He will tell you to skip this read-through. *Once is enough. Come on, we have shit to do!*

Get behind me, Belazybub. Truly I tell you, Editor: You will see or realize something on that second reading draft that you didn't see on the first pass.

This time you can have a pen in hand, but don't mark on the manuscript (because you might start fiddling with lines). Instead, jot down your global comments and questions on a separate piece of paper.

Step 3: Once you're done with the two reading drafts, answer the following prompts. Don't get mired on the line level. As you address these prompts, think about the continental plates of your manuscript: characters, plot/sequence of events, the overall structure.

- What did the second reading draft help you realize? What did you see that you didn't see before?

- Think about the structure and sequence of events. Is there a better architecture or arrangement? What might that look like?

- Should any big parts (whole paragraphs, pages, sections) be cut or moved? If so, why?

- What's missing? In a fully-realized version of this manuscript, what else would be on the page?

- Is there a better (perhaps later) place to begin the story? Is there a better place to end it?

- Think about character. What changes (or development) is needed?

> Always be on the lookout for opportunities and possibilities for the writer to explore. A question that starts with *What if* can crack a manuscript wide open.
>
> Other questions can be valuable as well. An editor does not have to have all the answers. Sometimes a keen observation or a well-posed question is better than a direct suggestion. Most times, it's better.

> Often the seeds of a great ending can be found in the beginning of a story.

- Are there any elements in the story that might be recirculated later?
- A good editor can amplify a story's assets. How can you make this story itself, only more so?

Step 4: At this point, you've made notes about the story, and you have answers to the prompts above. **Use the material from your notes and answers to write a message to the author communicating your global editing suggestions**. Be clear and constructive. Remember that your goal is to propel the writer into another draft, and if the writer feels lost or disheartened or full of self-loathing, they're not likely to do their best work. Refer to the model message "for global edits-only" provided in the "Correspondence" chapter, and make sure to end your message by addressing:

- What the author should do if they have questions
- What you would like to get back from the author, and
- A deadline, even if it's tentative

Editing with a Heavy Hand

Goal: To learn what it's like to make big moves in editing.

> Is it possible that Pound was thinking about his edits on this famous poem when he later said, "It's immensely important that great poems be written, but it makes not a jot of difference who writes them."?

When T. S. Eliot asked Ezra Pound to edit *The Waste Land*, Pound cut about half of it and stripped it of parody. When Thomas Wolfe delivered his manuscript for *Look Homeward, Angel* to his editor, Maxwell Perkins, it was 330,000 words. By the time Perkins was done with it, he had trimmed over 66,000 words.

Sometimes an editor works with a scalpel, sometimes a cleaver. Few editors have loved the cleaver more than Gordon Lish.

Lish was bold from the beginning. In 1969 he landed the job of fiction editor at *Esquire* on "nothing more than the strength of letter that he wrote to editor Harold T. P. Hayes," according to Alexander Nazaryan in *Newsweek*. During his tenure at *Esquire*, and later at Knopf and *The Quarterly*, Lish edited such luminaries as Barry Hannah, Joy Williams, Don DeLillo, and, most notably, Raymond Carver.

It was long rumored that Lish took a cleaver to Carver's work, especially his first two books, but the extent of his editing wasn't fully known until Lish sold his papers to the Lilly Library at Indiana University. In 1998, D. T. Max visited the library to write about the papers for the *New York Times Magazine*. Max saw "pages full of editorial marks—strikeouts, additions and marginal comments in Lish's sprawling handwriting. It looked as if a temperamental seven-year-old had somehow gotten ahold of the stories."

Lish made deep cuts, targeting introspection and anything that smacked of sentimentality. "When Lish got ahold of Carver," writes Max, "[his characters] stopped crying. They stopped feeling." Lish wasn't shy about making other changes, either. With Carver's second collection of stories, *What We Talk About When We Talk About Love*, Lish "rewrote ten of the thirteen endings."

After his second collection, Carver was renowned as a writer of gritty realism. For a while, Carver was grateful for Lish's editing, but later he resisted such aggressive incursions, and their relationship soured. When the truth came out about the heavy editing on Carver's early stories, reactions were mixed. In the *New York Times Book Review*, Stephen King called Lish's approach "a cheat." But in 2008, when Carver's widow published some unedited versions of his stories, Giles Harvey noted in the *New York Review of Books* that comparing the unedited stories with the edited versions only "pointed up the editorial genius of Gordon Lish."

WHAT WE TALK ABOUT WHEN WE TALK ABOUT LISH

Stripping a story to the gleaming bone. Direct suggestions, even re-writing. More than anything, a complete lack of timidity.

Which brings us to the reason we're talking about Lish—and Pound and Perkins, for that matter. Emerging editors tend to be timid. Often, they treat a manuscript with an abundance of trepidation, like it's a sweaty stick of dynamite. Why?

It might come from their belief about how writing works.

Here is the writing philosophy of a typical novice: A writer has an idea. The job of writing is to communicate that idea; the writer only has to find the right words. "We often discuss art this way," writes George Saunders in *The Guardian*. "[T]he artist had something 'he wanted to express,' and then he just, you know . . . expressed it. We buy into some version of the intentional fallacy: the notion that art is about having a clear-cut intention and then confidently executing same."

If you believe in this version of the intentional fallacy, of course you'll approach editing with trepidation, because you'll be worried about messing up the author's intent. *Every word is there for a reason*, students have told us in the past, even as they admit they can't see the reason for many of the words.

Let us suggest a different perspective on artistic creation, one shared by many experienced writers and editors: The writer comes up with something like an idea for a story (or a poem, or essay, or whatever), but it's not fully formed. Writing is the way the writer discovers the story, and then develops and deepens it. Writing isn't just about transmitting a preconceived intent; it's a way of figuring things out.

What does this mean for the editor? If you believe, as so many experienced writers do, that writing is a dynamic process of discovery, then the story on your desk is not a sacred expression of a writer's inviolable intent. It's a thing in the process of becoming, and it's your job to help it become itself. What we're talking about here is a mental shift from preservation to possibility. We're talking about becoming an intrepid editor.

How to do this? Start by playing with the cleaver. You might find that you like it. Or you might find that you're more comfortable with a whittling knife—and that's fine. Our goal here isn't to crank out baby Lishes. What is our goal? For you to view writing as discovery, which will permit you to make bigger moves as an editor, which will expand your editing capacity.

Practice

To Do

Pick one of the CPR Dummy stories in the appendix. Lish the hell out of it. Slash and strike out. Rewrite sentences, paragraphs, passages, the ending.

To Consider

1 Reflect on the experience of editing with a heavy hand. What was it like? How did it make you feel?

2 Was it good for the story? Was the end result better than if you had edited with a light hand?

3 How did this exercise change the way you think about editing, and how you will approach the practice in the future?

4 Consider the cases of Pound, Perkins, and Lish. Is it ethical to edit with such a heavy hand, or is it "a cheat"?

5 Is an editor's primary responsibility to the writer, or is it to the manuscript and its readers? Unpack your answer about that responsibility. What does it entail for your approach to editing?

Editing with the Body

Goal: To learn to pay attention to your "felt sense."

Bryan here. We had a piano in my house when I was growing up. Once a year, my parents would call in a tuner to open the old girl up, exposing her golden ribcage to the dusty light coming through the bay window. Most of the technicians used a tuning fork, but one guy tuned by ear. With a faraway look on his face, he'd plink a key, adjust a peg on the soundboard, plink the key again . . . repeating the process until he seemed satisfied before moving on to the next key.

"How do you know when it's right?" I asked him.

"When it feels right," he said without looking up from the piano.

That line makes me think of my mother, whose nervous system also seemed to be wired to the piano. She may not have had perfect pitch like the tuner, but whenever I hit a wrong note during my practice, she would let out an *Aaargh* like the note pained her. *Aargh* from the kitchen. *Aargh* from the sunroom. Once a ghostly *Aargh* floating through the heating duct.

My mother hates it when I tell that story (sorry, Mom), but my guess is that Gene Gendlin, psychologist and philosopher, would have appreciated her groans. Gendlin coined the term "felt sense" to talk about this kind of body-mind connection. For Gendlin, felt sense is a "kind of bodily awareness that can be used as a tool." Gendlin used this tool in psychotherapy, but it was composition scholar Sondra Perl who brought the tool into the writing classroom.

In her landmark book, *Guidelines for Composing*, Perl shows writers how to use felt sense to attend to intuition as well as cognition. As she writes in "Understanding Composing," the process of developing a felt sense for writing "begins with paying attention . . . to one's inner reflections and is often accompanied by bodily sensations."

You're familiar with the kind of bodily sensations she's talking about, even if you don't think you are. I'm willing to bet you feel something—some twinge or twang, an inner *Aargh*—when a writer bungles a line. "Think about it," urges Peter Elbow in the foreword to Perl's *Felt Sense: Writing with the Body*. "When we hear the 'offness' in a word we've used, we hear it, even if it's just slightly off."

Not everyone has the writerly equivalent of perfect pitch, but we all have an internal tuner that responds to the music of words. The more you read and write and edit, the more precise and sensitive your tuner will be—but regardless of your experience level, you have one.

Just as Perl applied Gendlin's practices to writing, we'll extend them to editing. The following exercise will help you "attend to [your body,]" as Perl puts it, "and discover just what these inchoate pushes and pulls, these barely formed preverbal yearnings or leanings are beginning to suggest to us."

Practice

To Do

(The following exercise is adapted from Guidelines for Composing *by Sondra Perl)*

Step 1: Tune into your body

Choose a manuscript (which can be one of the CPR Dummy stories from the appendix). Find a good place to edit. Only you can say what this means for you, but look for a setting that won't distract you from the manuscript or your reactions.

Settle in with the manuscript, a pen, and a blank piece of paper. Get comfortable. Take a minute or two to sit quietly. Mentally scan your body from your toes to your scalp. Hover over spots of tension or discomfort, and either adjust your physical position or consciously relax that part of your body. Go slow. Breathe easy. It might help to close your eyes.

Step 2: Tune into your mind (and clear it)

Ask yourself: What's trying to get my attention? What's in the way of editing right now? If you're anything like us, your mind is a gnat-cloud of worries and reminders and fantasies and recriminations. As each thought snags your attention, jot it down on the clean piece of paper. Don't dwell on any of the thoughts. You can deal with them later. For now, just offload them from your mind onto the paper.

Step 3: Take your first pass through the manuscript

Read slowly. Pay deep attention to the manuscript and to your internal tuner at the same time. Whenever you feel like something is "off" with the manuscript, make a mark. If you feel like it's a misstep on the word- or line-level, make a little x in that area. If the issue seems bigger—if there's a problem with structure or logic or character, for example—make a *. If you feel the energy leaving the prose, if you feel yourself getting bored, make a ~

Key

Line-level: x

Higher level: ★

Energy loss: ~

For this step, don't dwell on any of these off-notes. Just make your mark and keep reading to the end of the manuscript.

Step 4: Articulate

Bring your body and mind back to stillness. As outside thoughts attempt to snag your attention, jot them down on your sheet of paper so you can maintain your focus.

Go back to the beginning of the story. Read it again slowly, stopping at each mark. For each mark, write a note articulating your gut reaction for the writer. In other words, diagnose the cause of each twinge. *I understand that Chet needs to explain the situation to Julie, but since the reader already knows what happened, direct dialogue might not be the best fit here. What if you summarized this part of the conversation instead?* is more precise and constructive than *I got bored here.*

Here are some questions that might help you articulate your twinges:

- What's missing?
- What's extraneous? What could be cut?
- What questions come to your mind?
- What are the possibilities or opportunities here?
- Can you make a connection to an element of craft?

TWO CAVEATS

No matter how skilled you become, you're not going to be the right editor for every manuscript. Maybe you don't know enough about a particular genre, or there isn't enough overlap between your sensibility and the writer's sensibility. If you feel a twinge that lets you know you're the wrong editor for a manuscript, tell the writer. There's no shame in it, and you'll probably save both of you a lot of pain.

Finally, don't trust your intuition too much. Make a habit of questioning your gut. Ask yourself, "Am I going *Aargh* here because something is actually off, or because I'm unfamiliar with this move? Or is this twinge coming from my implicit bias?" Questioning your intuition is a good way to grow as a reader and editor, and to keep your tuner in tune.

To Consider

1 How did this go?

2 What happened as you tried this method? Any breakthroughs? Any brick walls?

3 How might you alter this process to better fit your sensibility next time?

Selection and Sequencing

Goal: To incorporate cutting and reordering into your editing practice.

Eudora Welty, the legend goes, used scissors to cut her stories into strips and spread them out on her long kitchen table. There she would rearrange the strips until they came together in a way that satisfied her, at which point she would attach the strips to each other with safety pins.

Picture it: silver pins gleaming in the lamplight, scraps of paper rustling on the table, Welty holding her breath so she doesn't disturb the order as she stitches a curtain of white. Not just a captivating image but a lesson for us all: You can play with order. The original sequence of a story is not sacred. Lines, paragraphs, sections, chapters—these can all be rearranged or cut, which are two operations performed by experienced editors. With the following exercise, you'll get a chance to focus on selection and sequencing.

Practice

To Do

This exercise works best with a hard copy of a manuscript. Here's what you'll need: scissors, glue, a copy of a manuscript (for this exercise, we recommend the CPR Dummy Story "We All Just Pretended to Like it So You Wouldn't Flunk Us" from the appendix), and a few sheets of blank paper to glue those strips onto. Oh, and you'll also need some space to spread out those strips.

The steps:

1 Read the manuscript.

2 Cut it up into parts. (If you're using "We All Just Pretended to Like it So You Wouldn't Flunk Us," you probably want to make each entry its own slip.)

3 Rearrange the slips. Play with the order.

4 Feel free to move or remove sentences from individual slips. This exercise is as much about selection (and de-selection) as it is about sequencing.

5 When you're satisfied with the new order, glue the slips onto the blank sheets of paper. Or get crazy with some safety pins. Your choice. Just don't hurt yourself. The people in the ER will laugh if you roll in there with an editing injury.

To Consider

- Talk about the changes you made to the manuscript. What's your rationale?
- Describe the effect the old order might have had on a reader. Describe the effect the new order might have on a reader.
- How does the new order change the manuscript's meaning?
- What was it like to play with a manuscript in this way?
- How did the use of craft tools (scissors, glue, etc.) affect your editing process?
- How might your experience with this exercise influence the way you approach manuscripts in the future?

Editing with Lenses

Goal: To train your editing focus on a single aspect of the manuscript at a time.

An axiom from the world of sales: If you give someone two choices, they'll probably pick one. If you give them three choices, they'll say, "I have to think about it." If you give them four choices, they'll say, "Forget it, I'm fine with what I have." Our point: Trying to consider too many things at once can be paralyzing.

That point is valid for editing, too, which you may know if you've ever tried to "fix everything" in a single pass over a manuscript that needed a good deal of work. But how else are you supposed to go about it?

When the poet Tom Lux revised his own work, he used an approach he referred to as "lenses." He took multiple passes over a poem, but only focused on one aspect per pass. If he was reading the poem through the "cliché lens," for example, he only looked for clichés. Then he might take another pass with the "verb lens," looking for passive voice and questioning every verb ending in -ing (e.g. the dubious "looking" and "questioning" in this sentence). Then another pass with the "line break lens," and so on.

Lux's approach can be particularly useful for the emerging editor because it gives you a specific and limited job for each pass. As an added benefit, your understanding of the manuscript and its architecture will deepen with each reading draft, so that by the time you're done with this exercise, you'll see the bones of the manuscript more clearly than you could after the first or second read.

Practice

To Do

1 Pick a manuscript—a CPR Dummy story or a different one, your choice—and read it once without marking it up.

2 Pick your lenses. Some of your lenses might be editing operations (e.g. addition. If you pick the lens of addition, you might ask yourself questions like: What's

missing? What can be further developed? Where do I see opportunities?) Other solid lenses include clarity, cliché, sensory detail, subject lens, and verb lens, though you might want to try different lenses, depending on your manuscript.

3 If you're working on a hard copy of the manuscript, select a different colored marker for each of your lenses. If you're working on a digital copy of the manuscript, you can use a different text highlight color for each lens.

4 Go through the manuscript again slowly, employing one lens per pass, using the chosen color to highlight passages that should be changed. For each highlighted passage, write a corresponding suggestion to the writer in the margin (Remember: Half of the editing game is persuasion. If you want someone to make a change, tell them why you think it's a good idea.). For example:

> How about this phrasing? It's more concise, and I don't think any meaning would be lost.

Our point: ~~Trying to consider~~Considering too ~~many things~~much at once can be paralyzing.

5 Using what you learned in the chapter on correspondence, write a letter to the writer to accompany the marked-up manuscript.

> If you think multiple rounds of editing might be necessary, it's wise to give the writer a heads-up about this possibility early in the editing process. For a model of this heads-up, see the message in Correspondence: Initial Contact.

Just as it can be paralyzing to try to "fix everything all at once" as an editor, it can be paralyzing (or demoralizing, which has the same effect) for a writer to handle too many big jobs in a single revision. There is no editing law that says a writer only gets one swing at a revision. It's not uncommon for editors and writers to bat around drafts for multiple rounds, so be conscious of how many big jobs you give a writer at one time.

To Consider

1 What happened as you tried this method?

2 After all these passes, what did you notice about the manuscript's architecture or meaning that you didn't notice after the first pass?

3 What did this exercise teach you about editing, or about yourself as an editor?

4 What might you do differently next time? How might you alter this process for the next manuscript you edit?

Scalpel Edit

Goal: To practice the editing operations of cutting and rewording for the purpose of compression/concision.

Do you know how to make a balsamic glaze? You simmer some balsamic vinegar in a saucepan until it reduces to a silky, delicious oil. It still tastes like balsamic, only more so. Less water, more potent.

Reduction can make written work more potent, too. Here's a writer's trick: When you're absolutely, positively certain you're done with a manuscript—when you think it is polished and perfect—pretend an editor has demanded that you cut it by 10 percent. At first, you'll think there's no way you can do it, but you'll find a way. You might even end up cutting more than 10 percent. And 99 times out of 100, the manuscript is better for it.

But what to cut? How to trim? There's "more than one way to skin a draft," as Tony Tulathimutte writes in the article below.

"To the Quick"

I'll be brief. Most books contain too many words. For all that people bemoan the "snippetization" of prose and praise the "longread," length isn't a virtue in itself. As a chronically unterse writer who spent a year ripping two hundred pages from my novel, I've learned more than one way to skin a draft: merge scenes, murder characters, "start as close to the end as possible" (Kurt Vonnegut), quit writing altogether.

But the most useful and underrated technique is what's sometimes called the "scalpel edit": clipping and nipping your manuscript line by line. Once I started focusing solely on lowering the word count, everything looked baggy. My first draft contained the line: "Up to a certain degree he felt there was nothing wrong with disliking work," which ended up as: "Still, it beat real work."

So here's some tricks to keep things short. Start by eliminating pad words that are meant to yield greater precision or emphasis, but achieve the opposite. Consider downtoners like "nearly" and "almost": *He was almost insane with irritation.* "Insane" is obviously exaggerated, so "almost" only weakens it. Intensifiers like "very" and "extremely" signal that a stronger adjective or verb is required instead, so that *He was extremely confused* becomes *He was dumbfounded.* Ditto for "all at once," "in a flash," "without warning," "abruptly," "instantly," "suddenly," or "all of the sudden"—ironically, these drain away suddenness by giving the reader a heads-up.

Some constructions add nothing but vagueness: *She had a quiet kind of dignity* or *He made a sort of half-smile.* Not only do these inflate simple declarations—she was dignified, he half-smiled—they're also underconfident. Similarly, starting a sentence with "there are/is/were" is seldom necessary. My fix for both is to turn the object into the subject, leaving room for more detail: *His half-smile revealed his inflamed gums.*

Formality is another bloater. When writers worry about sounding plain, unceremonious, or dumb, they reach for polysyllables and unnecessary phrases. George Orwell reviles the use of "render inoperative" to replace "break," while David Foster Wallace cringes at people writing "utilize" instead of "use" or "at this time" instead of "now." Likewise, in literature, people abuse rhetorical devices, my least favorite of which is anaphora—when successive phrases begin with the same words. Many such passages, borrowing the rhythms of venerated writing ("It was the best of times, it was the worst of times"; "Love is patient, love is kind"), are praised as "strong" or "lyrical" instead of what they usually end up being: lazy and hollow, lending a ponderous refrain to a flimsy sentiment.

But informal and personal narration can be clunky too. In first-person prose, phrases that mark a statement's subjectivity—"I feel like," "I find that," "I tend to think," "in my opinion,"—mostly go without saying; they're implied, for example, in this piece. "Seem to" and "appear to" are also common eyesores—I once read a manuscript with the line "He was standing near what appeared to be a sink." Most speechy tics should be skipped: *The best thing about him is that he's funny* or *It was exactly this sort of thing that bothered him.* And dialect in fiction can be great, but it's still no excuse to meander: *Well, it was about, oh, say, the first warm doggone day of March some ten years back, when a body could see Ol' Man Higgins a-settin' and a-whittlin' out on his porch . . .*

Most writers develop pet strategies for tidying up. You'll probably recall Strunk and White's famous dictum to "omit needless words," and their prescriptions to avoid the passive voice, use parallel constructions, and so on. Mark Twain killed adjectives, Stephen King adverbs. But orthodoxy can lead you back into wordiness. Sure, adverbs can be vague, ham-fisted, and/or redundant— *"I need you," he said desperately*—but sometimes they're efficient. Here's one from Philip Roth's "The Conversion of the Jews":

> "The Catholics," Itzie said helpfully, "they believe in Jesus Christ, that he's God." Itzie Lieberman used "the Catholics" in its broadest sense—to include the Protestants.

Here, "helpfully" is ironic, and serves to distinguish the narrator's perspective from the characters' with just one word. And it's certainly better to say *He closed the door carefully* than *He closed the door with a great deal of care*—though you might also argue that *He eased the door shut* is better than both.

> Our note: Adverbs are best when they give the reader something unexpected, putting the sentence on tilt.
>
> For example, here's a useless, redundant use of an adverb: "I'm so happy!" she shouted merrily.
>
> Now here's a more interesting use of an adverb: "You're the best thing that ever happened to me," he said begrudgingly.

I know all this sounds like tweedy editorial nitpicking, and some filler can't ruin an otherwise great book—who could turn down one of Dickens's puff pastries? My finished novel is pockmarked with *almost*s. Still, beyond concentrating your prose, extreme concision can yield an individual style, not just for minimalists like Carver, but even for the prolix David Foster Wallace, with his devised signature shorthands ("w/r/t," "IYI"). Once I attained nirvana, I found myself replacing *near* with *by, and then* with either *and* or *then*, and the past progressive (*I was going*) with the past participle (*I went*).

Last thing: Don't worry too much about deleting until late in the process. An overlong first draft is normal and fine, but in revision, concision is a stylistic imperative second only to eliminating cliché. If you can reduce the manuscript's word count while preserving the meaning, it'll be objectively improved—a rare guarantee. The more you begrudge every word, syllable, and letter, the less readers will hate you.

TONY TULATHIMUTTE is the author of the novel *Private Citizens* and has received a Whiting Award and an O. Henry Award. He has written for *The New York Times, VICE, The New Yorker, The New Republic, N+1, Playboy, The Paris Review,* and elsewhere. He lives in New York.

THREE MORE TRIMMING TIPS FROM BRYAN & SARAH

Question every filter. Filtering is when something is presented through another character's senses. For example: *She watched the gray man cross the street* is filtered; *The gray man crossed the street* is not filtered. Filters are not always bad. Sometimes there's a good reason to use one. But if you can't find a good reason, cut it.

Watch out for "began." *He began to edge toward the door* is really the same as *He edged toward the door*, right? Most of the time, "began to" or "started to" can be excised.

Don't use two verbs (or verb phrases) when one will do. Usually, if you keep the second verb, it implies the first verb. *I took out my comb and ran it through his wet hair* could be shortened to *I ran my comb through his wet hair.*

Practice

To Do

Remember the trick about cutting 10 percent? That's what we'll ask you to do. Choose one of the CPR Dummy stories ("Evolution" is a good fit for this exercise) or another manuscript of your choice and start cutting.

Pro tip: Read it first without a pen in hand so you can get a sense of the whole before you start tossing out parts. On your second pass, even as you lock into the line-level, keep in mind how your tiny alterations affect the whole story. This is the real trick of editing: to be the hawk and the dachshund at the same time.

To Consider

1 What did you learn—from this article, and from doing a scalpel edit?

2 What surprised you about the reading or the exercise—positively or negatively?

3 What was the most challenging part of the exercise?

4 What questions do you still have about this kind of editing?

Crafting an Editing Philosophy

Goal: To discover what you believe about the craft of editing, and to articulate your beliefs for others.

Bryan here. The first time I applied for a teaching position, the application called for a teaching philosophy statement of two to three pages.

A few pages? I thought. *No problem.*

It wasn't until I put pen to paper that I realized how much I had to figure out about my own beliefs. What is the purpose of teaching? Why grade? What is the nature of knowledge? It wasn't enough to answer these questions like I was taking a multiple-choice test; I had to articulate why I believed what I believed.

I sweated over that essay for weeks. In draft after draft, I tested out my beliefs and explored their rationale. When at last I finished the statement, I was flooded with relief and a particular kind of satisfaction, the satisfaction of having figured something out.

I might have started writing that essay for the hiring committee, but along the way I saw how the exercise was making me a better, more intentional teacher. The last draft was for me, and for my students.

This is why we're inviting you to write a statement of your editing philosophy. It's primarily for your own development, though it's not a bad idea to share it with others.

Typically, I share my teaching philosophy with my students. If they know why I'm doing what I'm doing, they're more likely to engage in the class—or to transfer to a different teacher whose philosophy is a better fit with their own. Likewise, your writers and readers might appreciate knowing the methodology behind your madness.

The good news is that you're more prepared to write your editing philosophy statement than I was to draft my teaching philosophy. In working your way through this book, you've figured out your stance on many big questions. Also, we'll give you prompts. Like the model texts provided in the early chapters, these prompts are meant to be generative, not limiting. Springboards, not cages. If you want to take a stance on an issue that is not raised by our prompts, do so.

We'll also provide support in the form of model texts. The appendix includes editing philosophy statements written by undergraduate students. You might also consider the interviews in the case studies in which editors address many of these prompts.

One last thing: Your editing philosophy is a living document. It will evolve as you develop as an editor. As a good editor, you'll question and challenge yourself. In this way, you'll edit yourself.

Practice

To Do

Draft an editing philosophy statement. Feel free to use the prompts below to generate material and the model texts in the appendix to inform your writing.

1 The big question: What do you believe about editing—and why do you believe it?

2 What is the value of editing? Why edit?

3 What is the role and purpose of the editor?

4 What is a metaphor for the editor? *An editor is* _____.

5 Is the editor's primary responsibility to the writer, to the manuscript and its readers, or magazine/press?

6 Describe how a good editor operates.

7 What are the ethics of editing?

8 What do editors owe writers? How should an editor work with writers?

9 Describe (and rationalize) your approach or style.

10 How firm are your suggestions? How open are you to pushback from writers?

11 In the event of a disagreement between editor and writer, who should have the final say, and why?

Appendix

A note about these stories: They're not great. They're not supposed to be great. We wanted to give you something half-baked so you'd have a lot of editing opportunities. The good news is that you can do whatever you want to these stories, and no author will mind.

Dispatch from the Bunker

Greetings, Bunkerheads. This is Tuesday, April 4th, and I am your host, Dave, filing yet another dispatch from . . . The Bunker

[rising air sirens, staccato machine gun sound, wailing guitar overlay, male heavy-metal voice screaming "Welcome to the Bunker!"]

Okay, okay. This is a very special episode. An episode of truth. I am going to level with you. About everything. And then that's it, because this is the very last dispatch. I'm calling it a career. And to celebrate, I am opening a very special bottle of Basil Hayden's , which I had been saving for a very special occasion. It's probably ten years old. I'm going to mix up some old fashioneds and I'm gonna podcast some truth!

[sound of wrapping crackling open, cork coming out, bourbon splashing over ice, ice cubes clinking around glass, drinking]

Ah. Nice. Kind of sad. Not the occasion I was hoping for. But like we say: You don't get the apocalypse you want, you get the apocalypse you deserve.

[sound of drinking]

Speaking of which, I'm not going to be talking about an apocalypse today. If you're new to the show, here's how it works. I pick a doomsday scenario—Great Flood, Fire-Ant plague, meteor strike—and I tell you what kind of wasteland we'd be facing, and what it will take in terms of equipment and skills to hack it. But I'm not going to be doing that today, so if you're new, you probably want to stop listening now. Actually, if you're One of the Faithful, you probably want to stop listening now, too. Otherwise you'll hate me by the end of the episode. Go trawl through the trove of the previous, what, a hundred and ninety-two episodes. Jesus. That's a lot. I never thought it would last that long. But then, I'm also surprised it's over.

[sound of ice hitting teeth, sound of uncorking, burbling]

I gotta say, this bourbon, it's pretty special, but it doesn't taste Very Special. I gotta say, I expected more. But that's pretty much always the case, isn't it? I mean, when's the last time that something, anything, like, exceeded your expectations? Maybe that's just me, just my problem. Andrew used to tell me that I built things up too much. He said if there ever was an actual apocalypse, that I'd probably walk outside and say, That's it?

But now. I don't know. I think he's wrong about that. Hey, guys?

[drinking sound]

Guys. Andrew left me. It's been two weeks. Seventeen days, to be exact. He said he was sick of all the doom and gloom. Quote unquote. Guys, I should have seen it coming. All the signs were there. He'd been spending more and more time away from home, claiming that between the recording equipment and the post-apocalyptic paraphernalia that the apartment was getting a little too Howard Hughes-y.

He never supported me. Not really. Not even in the beginning, when we both lost our jobs. When I looked into podcasting, Andrew didn't want me to do it. He thought it was—to use his word—"gross." Especially the topic. He associated post-apocalyptic planning with extreme right-wingers, gun nuts and xenophobes, the kind of guys who are secretly rooting for a race war. Wingnuts. Kooks. I'm sure you've heard the terms, guys. I'm sure they have hurt you as they have hurt me. But even then, Andrew's protests were feeble. He had seen my plan, my projections. The projected income from advertising. From talking about product, then linking to product, then taking a cut on the back end when you guys buy it. From my own eventual line of Dispatch-branded products. He believed in my spreadsheets if not my vision. He claimed I was profiteering off of paranoia. Anyway, Andrew wanted to protest—he wanted it Duly Noted—but he wanted me to earn, too, so he didn't get in the way. That's what he would say when he cleared out of the apartment whenever I recorded. "I don't want to be in the way, Dave." Whenever I started recording, he would leave. Just flat-out leave. He said it was because he was too shy and self-conscious to have so much as a creaking footstep or the clink of a dish show up on the reel. He said, too, that he wanted to be surprised when he listened to the episode after it was done, but now I know that was all a lie. He was actually spending his time setting up a new apartment. Where, I don't know. He wouldn't tell me, which, I have to tell you, felt like a knife-strike to the gut with a carbon steel sawback blade. And then, right before he left, he showed me his phone—waved it at me—so that I could see at least two dozen episodes on his screen. All downloaded, all green. He had stopped listening to me months ago. My own apocalypse had been upon me, and I hadn't even known it. Even if I wanted to keep doing this show, guys, I wouldn't be qualified.

[drinking sound]

As it turned out, my projections were a little bit—ha—optimistic. Yes, okay, I'm making a living, but it's a pretty scrubby living. I'm kind of scraping by, to be honest. I shouldn't complain—I mean, I'm making a living by talking into a microphone a couple of hours a week—but still. My early projections, it turned out, were hilariously optimistic.

Before the crash, back when we had Real Jobs, Andrew and I had been accustomed to a certain lifestyle. That lifestyle has been downgraded a few notches. Several notches. Goodbye, house; hello, apartment near the VA. Goodbye, Infiniti with the excellent sound system; hello, trusty-but-rusty Civic. Goodbye, organic squash; hello, apples the size of monkeyheads that taste like dirty water.

After Andrew stormed out, I left the apartment. The sky was clear, the sun was obscene. I squinted and my eyes watered. I walked down past the VA. Past the scuffed plexiglass of the bus shelter. The guys waiting there, unmoving, like they were fishing. The wind ruffling their hair. The orderlies standing on the other side of the street, smoking. The wind, the wind. One guy on a bike, pushing into the wind with his head down. Grit all over the street. Where did it come from? The street looked like a dried-up creekbed. The street had never been swept. Maybe the city hoped the grit would fall into the potholes and fill them up. But in my experience, one problem does not solve another. A security guard wearing a windbreaker that was snapping like a flag. Low clouds, budging across the sky like bumper-to-bumper at 5:05 on Meridian. It was the first hit of spring warmth that made you crazy. Forty-eight degrees, the tang of ice still in the air, and the orderlies were out smoking in shirtsleeves.

I didn't know where I was going. All I knew was that if I stayed in the apartment I would end up breaking all the equipment. I had that tingly feeling that meant I was about to lose control. But I was sweating and dizzy from the sun so I sat down in the bus shelter where all these guys were congregated. They scooted over for me on the bench and once they did, I noticed they were all missing parts. Legs, hands, eyes. I stood up again and they unscooched. This took a while, as you can imagine. They were silent in a way that suggested they had been talking, and had paused at my interruption, and were waiting for me to leave before they started talking again. I saw Harold Fishbein. I said, Harold, give me your medicine for PTSD. He said, I have diabetes. I said, Harold, I'm just talking about a few pills here, not your whole stash, help me out. He said, Do you think you have PTSD? I said, Name one single person you know who doesn't have it. Harold says, I think I'm going to pray for you. I say, Harold, please, goddammit. Can you help me out or no? He said, Hush. I'm praying for you right now. Can you feel it?

I couldn't. And then I could and I didn't appreciate it. I could feel his pity all over me like a sticky blanket. I said, Shut up, Harold. Shut your fucking mouth. Well, by now, the other guys are grumbling. They want me to leave, I can tell. So what do I do? I turn on all of them. I said, A little advice, you sad fucks. Stop wearing your war jackets. That's such an obvious play for pity, and everyone resents it. Stop moping and muttering. So what you don't have legs or whatever. You look like tramps. Is that what you want? To look like tramps?

And one of them says, I fought for your freedom, man.

I said, Someone lied to you, you dumb fuck.

Harold stopped praying right then.

I'm not proud of that. I'm not proud of anything from that day, but for about a second I did feel better.

Let's take a break.

—back. I'm back. In my closet, where I'm hunched over a microphone and a laptop next to a garbage bag full of clothes that I was supposed to take to Goodwill like a year ago. Yep, that's the famed bunker. I'm not actually broadcasting through three inches of solid steel set in poured concrete buried in an undisclosed hillside in West Virgina. That, I'm afraid, is a fiction. The truth is that all that stands between me and the world is a half-inch of hollowcore door. It's dingy at the bottom. Andrew has a habit of nudging a door open with his foot at the same time he twists the knob.

Had a habit. He had that habit.

Though I guess he still has that habit, just . . . Fuck.

[drink]

This bottle was forty-five dollars. It's sad that it is my special bottle. I always imagined that my special bottle would be like two-hundred dollars. Some scotch that is aged in a peat bog until its original maker died of oldness or something. That's not how it worked out, though. I turned out to be the kind of guy who has to save a bottle of forty-five dollar bourbon, and then who ends up drinking it at a time like this. Ha. More doom and gloom.

Maybe this apocalypse will end. Maybe I'll find out that there is no post- apocalypse. There is no aftermath. It's just all math. All ongoing until there is no-going and no one left. What if the floodwaters don't recede? What if the meteors don't stop falling? What if the world is a cinder? No small, hardy band of survivors. Nothing to cultivate. What if it's just over? I suppose I lied again, guys. Today was a scenario after all: dealing with the apocalypse that never ends.

You know the thing I said earlier about PTSD? I think it's true. Because maybe the apocalypse has already happened, and none of us realize it. Maybe it happened so slowly that we didn't really realize it. Maybe someone hid it from us, like Andrew's new apartment (how the fuck did he scrape up a security deposit?). Maybe it was a million micro-pocalypses, none of them big enough to be noticed, but accumulating over time. The superstorms, hospital bombings, mine collapses, terrorist attacks, active shooters, the retributions, the endless retributions—a million patches in a crazy-quilt apocalypse. A million natural and social mini-strokes.

Too many metaphors. I picked that habit up from Andrew. It's funny, I used to ride him for that habit. Pick one metaphor, I'd tell him. "If one's good, three are better," he'd say. And I'd scowl, and he'd grin and toss in one more metaphor, and I'd pretend to throttle him—and now look at me with his stupid habit. Look at me.

I'm dying. We're all dying. Yes. I think that's true. We're going extinct. I'm afraid we've passed the tipping point, the point of no return, we've Evel-Knieveled across the Rubicon and everything has accelerated and, guys, I'm afraid . . .

[drinking sound]

Wake up, Dave. That's one of the last things he said to me. He was like: Earth to Dave. You are not a survivalist. You are a guy with a Honda Civic. You are a guy with a burgeoning Hoho problem. If you went out for a hike, you'd be lost in about eight seconds. You are allergic to every weed known to man. The last time we camped, your eyes got so itchy and you rubbed them so much you scratched your cornea. He goes: You are living a lie.

Well, not anymore, Andrew. Not any—

Okay. I'm playing the victim here. I said I was going to be honest, so I'll be honest. The truth is, he tried to be cool, saying that we could be friends, and I said why would I be friends with a parasite? Then I made sucking sounds, like a leech. He said, Dave, you don't mean that. I said, If the shoe fits. He said, I really don't want to end it like this. We can just go our separate ways. That's when I pushed him. I—geez—I shouldn't have pushed him. That was wrong. It was just. I wanted him to push me back. I wanted to fight. Really fucking have it out. Because I think a part of me thought, you know, if we can blow out all these bad feelings, get it all out in the open, maybe the storm will pass, you know? But he didn't. He just said Ow. And: God, the bookshelf got me right in the ribs. And I said, Sorry, which was a mistake, too, because then I was emotionally off- balance and Andrew was always a judo-master at arguing, and that was the moment he chose to whip out his phone.

[sound of something getting knocked over, followed by soft cursing off-mike]

Question. Here's a question. Can you bring something about by preparing for it? Maybe we should stop, you know, stockpiling. Maybe we're summoning the end. We think we're about survival, but maybe the truth is that we're a death cult. It's like swimming through quicksand—the thing you think is saving you is dragging you down. But, guys. We can stop. Let's stop. I am stopping. Andrew, if you're listening, this is me, stopping.

We All Just Pretended to Like It So You Wouldn't Flunk Us

Teaching Evaluation Comments from Polly Tudor's Class for Stuffed Animals

Section 01 | M,T,W,R,F, Sa, Su | 4:00-Whenever Mom has Dinner on the Table

Never once saw a syllabus. Did this class even have objectives?

Good individual help. Lots of personal attention. Lots.

Zero time management skills. Often made mistakes during class. Sometimes cried about it. Took forever to grade.

She might be superinteligent or whatever, but what good is that if she can't explain shit in a way that makes sense? Her notes on the board were always cluttered/confusing/looked crazy.

I seriously love Miss Poley. You never knew what was going to happen in the classroom and I don't think she did, either. That kept us alert! Along with the snowcaps she hid under the bed.

That vow. Uggggggghhhhh.

Real passion for her subject (subjects?) and her students. I, for one, like the hugs. Also the tangents. Some people (like Mr. Grumpus and whats-his-face, that new kid) thought they were so effing clever, getting her off track with questions about her personal life, but if you ask me, that was the track.

MIZZ POLLY IS COOL 5/5 WOULD RECOMMEND. LOSE THE ROMPER, THO. NOT UR BEST LOOK.

I think the instructor's mind is sometimes elsewhere? Obvious she is stressed out & the course suffers slightly.

Course was better early on, when Miss Polly was chill. Still not sure why she made the decision to get freakishly intense, but it affected my experience negatively.

(Response left blank)

So many uncomfortable moments. Like the time Miss Polly's dad knocked on her door and she screamed Slut! Slut! at him until he opened the door just wide enough to push in a gift, a plush toad, and then she kicked the door shut, nearly pinching his fingers off. Or the time when she called Betsy Wetsy to the board and grilled her until she pissed herself. Anyway, this class is the #1 reason I'm transferring. Good luck running this shit show without my tuition dollars.

Miss Poly is awesome! She has a great personality, though maybe too intense and scattered for some. If she makes you take a vow, just think, hey, I say the Pledge of Allegiance all the time. Her vow is just like that, except you're pledging your loyalty to the class, plus the end part about hoping to die in a fire if you break the vow. Otherwise, pretty much the same. So just say it, or things will go very hard on you.

Fuck this school.

Super caring. I had some "difficulty" with a fellow student a couple of weeks ago, and Miss Polly took it on herself to counsel me. At first I was like, Why even pretend to care, bitch? You didn't care when you humiliated me at the board. But Miss Polly, she listened to me. She let know that my fellow student was a Major Whoremonger and that zero of my difficulty was my fault. She told me she had always cared, that she had only pushed me at the board on account of my huge potential. Then we cried together. She stroked my hair until I fell asleep. (Don't worry—she sleeps with all her students. Even Mr. Grumpus before he ghosted. That freaky toad, too.)

NO ONE WANTED YOR DISGUSTING HUGS MISS POLLY, WE ALL JUST PRETENDID TO LIKE IT SO YOU WOULDN'T FLUNK US.

(Appears to be a drawing of some kind. Scissors, maybe?) <u>Follow the evidence</u>.

Dear Administration or Whomever Reads These Things: Look into the disappearance of Mr. Grumpus. Miss Polly said that he dropped out, but like no one has seen him around the closet for a month, not since the day he refused to take the vow.

(Response entirely scribbled out.)

Some teachers say they have an open door policy, but Miss Polly means it. You could go to her anytime. Night or day, man. If you opened up to her, she would reciprocate. Like a

Real Person, like you were both Real People, you know? Like when I told her that everyone was taking someone to the Sweethearts Dance except for me, and she told me how she had accidentally set the dinner table for three and her mom picked up the third plate and winged it against the wall, but it (the plate) was Corelle and didn't break (SEE ATTACHED—ANSWER KEEPS GOING ON NEXT PAGE) but the throw hurt her mom's shoulder so bad that she (the mom) had to pour her wine left-handed, which led to spilling and some giggle-snorting, and then they both pretended to be left-handed all night. And then she (Miss Polly) gave me a sad smile, and then dressed me in a new outfit, which made me crazy with confidence. In conclusion, I took Betsy Wetsy to the Sweethearts Dance. P.S. I wish I could do something for Miss Polly to say thank you. Please give her a raise.

The math problems were stupid and unnecessary. So what if they're drawn from real life? they didn't help me and no one liked them. Also, took too long to return tests. Plus, she totally murdered Grumpus. One night I heard this snip, snip so I peeked out of the closet to see that bitch taking her mom's big scissors (which she is not allowed to use and she knows this) to Grumpus's buttons. Then his ears. Then his toes. Etcetera. Etcetera. Grumpus! Her oldest friend! (p.s. I know this form is anonymous. If you interrogate the class to find the witness, you will be in breach of contract, and also I will stonewall like a motherfucker. If she did Grumpus like that, who knows what she would do to a random snitch ~~who was given to her by her father as a guilt-gift~~.) ←NOT A CLUE. IGNORE THAT SHIT.

Is it a crime to be too intense, too passionate? If so, lock Miss Pollly up in the Jail of Good Teaching and throw the key into the Sea of Stupidity. To those who would tell her, "Get a life/friends your own age," I say: She dedicated herself to you, my friend, to all of us. She took that vow, too. And did she not enliven our lives on a daily basis? Was she not a spark in an otherwise ~~dim twilight~~ dusk-hued existence? I, for one, give mighty thanks for—

(handwriting too cramped at bottom of box to read the rest of response)

Evolution

A later version of this story was published in Sou'wester

Deciphered from cuneiform, this is the earliest known example of a break-up letter.

Dear Lucy,

What's up? Not much here. You're probably wondering why I'm writing a letter. If I know you—and after sharing your cave for a month, I think I do!—right now you're probably scratching your cute temple like what the heck? Ock is writing a letter? Ock LAUGHS at letter-writers, then says something witty like, "Make yourself useful," which is funny because he's just torn off their arms and is already carving the bone into spearheads.

Well, that was the Old Ock. New Ock has a different perspective. No doubt you've noticed that I've been standing a little more upright lately. As painful as that adjustment was at first, as foolish as I felt for "putting on airs," as my snorting father said, those few vertical inches have changed my worldview.

Literally. Now, instead of constantly looking at cracked mud and mammoth scat and your breasts, my view soars over treetops, stars, and your breasts.

These new sights put New Ock in mind of big and distant things. The horizon. The future. The whole deal between men and women. A view like this is enough to put even a man like Ock in a letter-writing mood.

Ah, but listen to me go on. If Dr. Ur was looking over my shoulder right now, he'd say that I was avoiding the real subject of this letter. Then again, if Dr. Ur was looking over my shoulder, he'd find himself with a bloody nub for an elbow, and me writing with a dripping shank of his forearm. Ha! But still, Dr. Ur would have a point, so let me get to mine. In a minute.

First, Lucy-in-the-sky, I need you to understand how much I have changed. For Old Ock, the day-to-day existence of hunting mammoths and gathering soft leaves to wipe our bottoms was a very full life. New Ock picks up his spear in the morning and thinks, *Is this it? Is this all there is?* Hunting used to thrill me. Now I just want to get it over with as quickly as possible so I can come home and figure out a hobby.

Mammoths, it turns out, are surprisingly dumb and easy to hunt once you straighten up. You see that they're basically clumsy, overgrown bears with no claws. It takes them about two minutes to sweep their tusks around. "Look UP!" I keep telling the other guys, but they just keep scuffling around its hooves, stabbing blindly up into its belly fur. In all the dust and hunched-over confusion, they mainly succeed in spearing each other, and, occasionally, themselves.

Eventually I get disgusted and walk over to punch a spearhole behind the mammoth's ear.

The guys cheer, then sit down to pack boiling mud into their spear wounds, which they blame on the mammoth. "Man, did you see that guy? His tusks were everywhere."

I tell them that straightening up, just a little, would make their job a whole lot easier and pain-free, but they scoff. Straightening up is not for them, they tell me. The sun gets in their eyes. It hurts their spines. And besides, if this posture was good enough for their fathers, it's good enough for them. Which makes me think of my own father, what he said when he first caught a glimpse of my straight back: *What, you're too good for me now?*

"I've always been too good for you, Dad!" is what I wanted to say, but I didn't. Dr. Ur says that showed good restraint, a real sign of evolution, but I kind of wished I had popped my father's mouth with the butt of my spear. That's what Old Ock would have done. Evolution has its downside, I guess.

Can you see how much I've changed? I'm not the same Ock you fell in love with. I still "hunt," but I don't feel like hunting defines me. I write letters now. And not even with a bone; with a *reed*.

I wouldn't blame you a bit if you didn't want to be with me anymore, Lucy-Goose. I can picture you now, pressing your lips together in cute concern for new Ock, thinking, *Nuh-uh. No way. I didn't sign on for this deal!*

You're right. It wouldn't be fair to expect you to stand by me when the deal has changed so much. That would be a real "bait and switch," which is what my unevolved father calls the trick where he sets out a scrap of meat, and, when a lizard appears, he whacks it with a switch.

As unfair as that is to the lizard, it would be doubly unfair for you, sweet Lu, which is why I refuse to do it.

I'm big into fairness now, as you can probably tell. While I used to think of might and right as identical twins, now I'm not so sure. Before I straightened up, I thought that just because I could pull off a letter-writer's arms meant that it was okay to do so. "It's not like it'll hurt the tribe," my father would tell me. "Those guys don't even gather leeks. And during a hunt, they always stay behind with the women." This is where he would tap his sloping forehead. "One more reason to tear off their arms."

Now, though, when I think about yanking limbs, a dark cloud forms behind my eyes. The same dark cloud is forming right now, I assume because I love you so much and yet, for the sake of fairness, am forced to say: let's take a step back here. Let's spend some time apart. Let's take a real clear look at ourselves and who we are becoming. Respectively.

If you think that sounds like Dr. Ur, well, ha ha, you're right. He gave me those lines, but when he did, he was just helping me realize what I was already thinking. Helping people realize things is apparently a gift that comes with being "born erect" (a phrase that Dr. Ur always says with a leer, though I don't know why).

But Dr. Ur is not so gifted that he can do all my realizing for me, so I have to go away from the village to spend some time by myself, which is another one of my ideas that just happened to come out of his mouth.

Maybe one day New Ock and Lucy can get together again with a clear-eyed understanding of ourselves and each other, though, now that we're on that subject, don't chase me, I'll chase you. If and when that time comes. More if than when.

If you want to see other guys, I guess I can't stop you. Just don't go out with any of my hunting buddies. Or any letter-writers. Or—God, I hope this goes without saying, but just in case it can't—my father. He'll probably ask you out, or set out a little scrap of your favorite meat, so be prepared.

Other than that, you're free, baby!

My only regret is that I don't get to see your tears of gratitude spilling onto this part of the letter, because I've already left the village.

If your gratitude tears won't stop, go talk to Dr. Ur. He always asks about you. You might be happy to know that we spent most of our time talking about you. In fact, in our last session, right after he told me what I was thinking in terms of leaving the village, he said he'd be happy to help you with your "rebound" at a big discount.

I hope you don't think that he's sending me away so he can get in your loincloth. He specifically told me he was not doing that. And—get this—he brought it up himself! I didn't even have to ask. Clever Dr. Ur, always one step ahead of me.

Lefty-Lucy, wish me luck in my hunt for understanding—between Ock and self, between Ock and woman—though I doubt I'll need it. My father thinks there are no answers, and Dr. Ur tells me I may have to spend years in the wilderness before I figure anything out, but this is one area where I have an advantage over both of them. Has my father ever willed himself into an evolution? Has Dr. Ur?

No. Only Ock.

Only Ock is asking these big questions, and I have reason to be confident that the answers will come soon. Looking at the stars written in the sky, I feel so close already. Understanding can't be more than one more evolution away.

Your friend always,

Ock

Editing Philosophy Statements: Student Examples

Chelsea Yedinak

Editing is the process by which a promising story fulfills its promise. All good stories need good writers, but they also need good editors. An editor is someone who cares about a story but has some measure of distance from the personal process of writing. They are able to see its flaws and its successes more clearly than the author because of that distance.

Their primary responsibility is to the manuscript and its readers. Sure, without the magazine/press, there would be no way for the manuscript to be published and reach its readers. But ultimately, without manuscripts and readers, the magazine/press cannot survive. The writer is certainly integral to the publishing equation, but they are not the editor's primary responsibility. They owe the writer patience, politeness, and understanding, because they have been entrusted with the writer's personal creation. In working with a writer, editors should ensure that they stay true to the writer's intentions and message. If they are unsure of the writer's intention, they should ask.

Editors are not co-authors, nor should they try to be. When I edit, I strive not to take too heavy a hand to a manuscript. I think small suggestions and questions at key points can work just as well as paragraphs of comments in the margins. My suggestions are always flexible and I'm open to pushback. Just as I might have my rationale for suggesting a change, writers have their own rationale for their work. At the end of the day, it is the author's story, and in most cases, they should have the final say. My edits are not the focus of the reader, the author's story is. As an editor, I want to be invisible but invaluable.

Mackenzie Thompson

Remember the "cool aunt" from the movies you watched as a kid? You know, the one who lets the kids eat dessert for breakfast and tells them stories about her wild teenage days? She offers guidance and support, but she isn't the person to provide discipline. In my opinion, that's what an editor does, too. My job as an editor is not to tell a writer what I believe is right or wrong with their piece, or to impose my own ideas on a writer. Rather, as an editor, I offer support and guidance to help a piece become what it is trying to be.

Through this, editors and writers collaborate to make the piece the best it can possibly be, which ultimately benefits the literary world as a whole.

Similarly, I believe that the aforementioned idea is the purpose of editing: to make manuscripts the best that they can be. Writers are the communicators of society and are responsible for information and ideas that are spread in societies and cultures through media. Editors are responsible for making sure that the information being communicated is clear and relatable and, in some cases, ethical, depending on the context of the piece. This is a responsibility that I am proud to accept and dedicate my time to.

This is not to say that these are the editor's only responsibilities or duties. Truthfully, I don't believe that there is a clear-cut path to what the editor's responsibilities are. They can vary based on the project. For instance, if I am editing a technical document, I may look for different attributes in a document than I would if I were editing a short fiction piece. I believe that a good editor operates on a case-by-case basis, yet in an efficient, constructive way.

I believe that editors owe constructive feedback and respect to writers, because even though we are editors, many of us are writers, too. We must remember that we are all human beings with important stories to tell.

Lydia Gentry

I BELIEVE THAT EDITORS SHOULD HELP THE AUTHOR MAKE THEIR MANUSCRIPT REACH ITS FULLEST POTENTIAL.

The primary purpose of an editor is to help the author nurture their manuscript until it is fully realized. Editors should not rewrite or repurpose the work; instead, they should work closely with the writer to ensure that the piece the writer had envisioned comes to life on the page. Editors have a unique advantage over the average reader because they have a direct line of contact with the author—a communication that should not be ignored or overlooked in order to get to the essence of the manuscript as the author intended.

I BELIEVE THERE SHOULDN'T BE AN UNEVEN POWER DYNAMIC BETWEEN THE AUTHOR AND THE EDITOR.

In many author-editor relationships, I have noticed a sense of superiority in one or both parties. However, it is my belief that the relationship should be a symbiotic one. The editor relies on the author to produce solid work, while the author relies on the editor to tease out weaknesses in the manuscript that they themselves may have overlooked.

I BELIEVE THAT HONESTY IS THE BEST POLICY.

Editors have an obligation to their authors to be honest. Always. The editor should always address every element of the manuscript that they believe could be improved upon with politeness and respect. If they fail to do so, they actually damage the author's work by forgoing the possibility for honest change. Likewise, the author has an obligation to respond to the editor's commentary in an open manner, lest resentment and tension build up. This is also a detriment to the manuscript, as writing cannot flourish in a hostile environment.

I BELIEVE IN WORKING CLOSELY WITH THE WRITER IN MANY DIFFERENT WAYS.

People communicate in a variety of different ways. I believe that the editor should be able to work with the author in any way that best serves frank, open communication. This could be email, phone calls, or meetings in person where geographically possible. Going the extra mile to communicate with the author fosters a healthy working relationship in which both parties are mutually benefitted.

I BELIEVE THAT WRITERS ARE NOT DISPOSABLE.

There is only one writer and only one manuscript. Editors must not see writers as a commodity, but as indispensable sources of knowledge and creativity.